SAMUEL PEPYS ESQRE

1. Mr Pepys by Hales

RICHARD BARBER

UNIVERSITY OF CALIFORNIA PRESS

PUBLISHED BY UNIVERSITY OF CALIFORNIA PRESS
BERKELEY · LOS ANGELES · NEW YORK

PRINTED IN GREAT BRITAIN BY BUTLER & TANNER LTD, FROME AND LONDON

ISBN 0 520 01763 3
LCCC NO: 70–123622

Acknowledgements

This exhibition could not have taken place without the assistance of the editors of the new edition of *Pepys' Diary* and of the keepers and curators of the various collections to whom we are indebted for loans. In particular, I should like to thank Mr Robert Latham, principal editor of the *Diary*; Mr Oliver Millar, Deputy Surveyor of the Queen's Pictures; Dr R. W. Ladborough and Mr D. Pepys Whiteley of the Pepysian Library, Magdalene College; Mr Peter Thornton and Mr Claud Blair of the Victoria and Albert Museum; Mrs Philippa Glanvill of the London Museum; Professor W. A. Armstrong; Dr McDonald Emslie; Mr Ronald Lee; and Mr Colin Sizer of the Wellcome Historical Museum; all of whom have given most useful advice. The staff of the National Portrait Gallery have been unfailingly helpful, and Mrs Maureen Hill has coped admirably with the somewhat unorthodox problems of organising the assembly of a seventeenth century interior.

It has been a special privilege to work with Miss Julia Trevelyan Oman, to whose tireless enthusiasm and unflagging imagination the exhibition owes its real character. Finally, as one among many Pepysian enthusiasts, I acknowledge with gratitude the opportunity offered by Dr Roy Strong to recreate a tangible glimpse of his period and surroundings.

Contents

Exhibition designed by

JULIA TREVELYAN OMAN

Foreword

Seven years ago the National Portrait Gallery staged the first of its biographical exhibitions, *The Winter Queen.* Four years later in 1967 came *Mr. Boswell* and now *Samuel Pepys Esq*^{re}. Each time an attempt has been made to explore, within the limited confines of our exhibitions area, means of successfully evoking a personality of the past. Pepys has presented special problems in that by the terms of his own will none of his personalia, including the celebrated *Diary*, can be lent from Magdalene College. In spite of this we have been able to gather together a formidable array of pictures, portraits, drawings, furniture, books, music and other material to re-create Pepys the man.

The main aim of the exhibition has been to cover the actual years of the *Diary* itself, its personalities and events as seen through the eyes of Pepys himself, and finally to catch glimpses of him in the setting of his own home. In this sense the emphasis of the exhibition is on the domestic as against the public aspect of his life.

The research and catalogue has been carried out by Mr Richard Barber with admirable enthusiasm and precision and the exhibition has been designed by Miss Julia Trevelyan Oman. To her the exhibition owes its very special character of imaginative historical observation giving back to objects their connection with life as it was once lived in another age.

Finally to the owners, both public and private of all the items lent to this exhibition, we owe a debt which can shortly be expressed by the fact that without their kindness there would be no *Samuel Pepys Esq*^{re}.

ROY STRONG

Chronology

	BIOGRAPHY	POLITICS	ARTS AND LITERATURE
1633	February 27: Born at Salisbury Court off Fleet Street, fifth child of John and Margaret Pepys		
1642	Sent to Huntingdon on outbreak of war. Attends Huntingdon Grammar School	August 22: Outbreak of Civil War	
1646	Goes to St Paul's School	May 5: Charles I surrenders to Scots	
1649		January 30: Charles I beheaded	Hobbes: *Leviathan* published
1651	Entered at Trinity Hall, Cambridge; transfers to Magdalene	January 1: Charles II crowned at Scone	
1652		June: First Anglo-Dutch war begins	
1653		December 16: Oliver Cromwell becomes Protector	Lely: *Oliver Cromwell* painted
1654	March: Takes B.A. degree. Soon afterwards enters Montagu's service in London	April 5: Treaty of Westminster ends Anglo-Dutch war	
1655	Marries Elizabeth St Michel		
1656	About this time, becomes Clerk to George Downing, Teller of the Receipt in the Exchequer		Davenant: *The Siege of Rhodes* performed
1658	March 26: Successful operation for removal of kidney stone by Mr Turner c. August: Moves to Axe Yard, Westminster, opposite Whitehall palace	September 3: Oliver Cromwell dies	
1659	May: Pepys joins Mountagu's squadron in the Baltic	March: Mountagu sent with fleet to Baltic May 25: Overthrow of Richard Cromwell August: Mountagu returns from Baltic, but royalist rising suppressed before his arrival October 12: Fall of Rump Parliament December 26: Parliament reassembles	
1660	January 1: Pepys begins to keep diary March 23: Pepys joins fleet as Mountagu's secretary May 11: Fleet sails to Holland to fetch Charles II May 17: Pepys sees Charles II at Hague May 27: Mountagu created Knight of the Garter (earldom in July) May 30: Pepys reckons his estate at £80 July 13: Pepys obtains patent as Clerk of the Acts to the Navy; moves to Seething Lane July 17	January 1: Monck leads army south from Scotland April 25: Newly elected Parliament meets and invites Charles II to return; Monck and Charles II already in secret agreement May 23: Charles sails for England, landing at Dover May 25	October: Official re-opening of London theatres. First professional appearance of actresses Lely begins series of 'Windsor beauties'
1661	Chosen younger brother of Trinity House Appointed Commissioner for Tangier May 30: Estate worth £500	April 23: Coronation of Charles II	Lely appointed court painter Davenant opens Lincoln's Inn Fields Theatre, Portugal St
1662	May 30: Estate worth £630	May 19: Act of Uniformity, re-establishing Anglican Church	Royal Society granted charter, July 15

	BIOGRAPHY.	POLITICS	ARTS AND LITERATURE
1663	May 30: Estate worth £726 November 18: Pepys writes 'a great letter of reproof' to Lord Sandwich over the latter's scandalous love-affair with Miss Beck		Theatre Royal, Vere St, opens, May 7
1664	May 31: Estate worth £930		
1665	February 15: Elected Member of the Royal Society March 20: Appointed Treasurer of Tangier Committee June: Negotiates marriage of Lord Sandwich's daughter Remains at London during much of plague, removing to Woolwich on August 31 June 4: Estate worth £1,400	February 22: Second Anglo-Dutch war begins June 10: Plague reported in the City June 29: Court leaves London	
1666	May 30: Estate worth £5,200 September 5: Pepys' home in Navy Office narrowly escapes fire November 8: Appointed Surveyor-General of Victualling November 17: Writes 'great letter to the Duke of York' on the 'ill-condition of the Navy'	February 1: Court returns to London after plague September 2–5: Great Fire of London	Lely begins series of 'Flag-officers'
1667	May 31: Estate worth £6,900 October: Begins to prepare defence of Navy against Parliamentary critics	March 21: Secret treaty with France June 12: Dutch burn English fleet in Medway July 21: Peace of Breda August 30: Fall of Lord Clarendon	Milton: *Paradise Lost* published
1668	March 5: Three-hour speech in defence of Navy Board before Parliament; much praised by hearers October 25: Pepys' *amour* with Deb Willet discovered by his wife		
1669	Discontinues diary due to failing eyesight July–October: Tour in France and Holland November 10: Death of Elizabeth Pepys		
1670		May 22: Secret Treaty of Dover (Franco-English alliance)	
1672		January 2: Exchequer payments suspended – many bankruptcies March 17: Third Dutch War November 17: Shaftesbury becomes Lord Chancellor	
1673	June 18: Appointed Secretary to the Admiralty November: Elected M.P. for Castle Rising	March 29: Test Act excludes Catholics from office June 12: Duke of York resigns as Lord High Admiral because of Test Act	
1674	February 17: cleared of charges of being a Roman Catholic		
1675			Rebuilding of St Paul's begun
1676	February 1: Appointed Master of Trinity House Governor of Christ's Hospital		
1677	Elected Master of the Clothworkers' Company		
1678	December: Pepys' clerk accused of being accessory to murder of Sir Edmund Godfrey	July 16: End of Third Anglo-Dutch War	

	BIOGRAPHY	POLITICS	ARTS AND LITERATURE
1679	March: Elected M.P. for Harwich March 21: Charged with selling naval secrets to France; imprisoned in Tower for six weeks. Still suspected of being a Catholic. Resigns as Secretary to Admiralty July 9: released on bail Moves to York Buildings, on site of Adelphi		
1680	February 12: Cleared of charges against him October: Takes down Charles II's account of his escape after the Battle of Worcester, 1651		Purcell appointed organist of Westminster Abbey
1682	May 5: Escapes shipwreck off mouth of Humber on voyage to Scotland with Duke of York		
1683	July 28: Appointed secretary to Tangier expedition under Lord Dartmouth; sails August 9. December 6 to February 26, 1684, visits Spain	October 4: London loses Charter	
1684	March 29: Returns to England June: Appointed Secretary for Admiralty Affairs December 1: Elected President of the Royal Society	Duke of York reappointed Lord High Admiral	
1685	Carries canopy at James II's coronation April: Elected M.P. for Harwich May 20: Installed Master of Trinity House May 30: Deputy Lieutenant for Huntingdonshire Reelected President of the Royal Society	February 6: Charles II dies October 18: Louis XIV revokes acts of religious tolerance. Huguenots emigrate on a large scale	
1686	Special commission set up on Pepys' recommendation to do work of Navy Office		
1687			Newton's *Principia Mathematica* published
1688		Declaration of Indulgence reissued, May 4 November 5: William of Orange lands in England December 11: James II attempts to escape December 19: William of Orange enters London December 25: James II flees to France	
1689	February 20: Resigns office as Secretary for Admiralty Affairs	February 12: Declaration of Rights April: William and Mary crowned	Purcell: *Dido and Aeneas* performed
1690	June 25: Committed to Gatehouse 'on suspicion of being affected to King James' June 30: Released on grounds of ill health October 15: Cleared of charges and released from bail		
1693	Compiles first catalogue of library		
1694		Bank of England founded	Kneller begins 'Hampton Court beauties'
1698	Sends John Jackson on tour of Italy and Spain		
1699	April 27: Made Freeman of City of London		
1701	Retires (c. June) permanently to Hewer's country house at Clapham		
1702		March 8: William III dies	Earl of Clarendon's *History of the Great Rebellion* published
1703	January 26: Dies at Clapham, aged sixty-nine		

Introduction

This exhibition is the portrait of one man Samuel Pepys, diarist, musician, bibliophile, theatre-lover, amateur of science and all curious knowledge, by profession administrator of the Navy, by inclination man of the world. It is not conceived as a biography, laboriously and lovingly collecting scattered traces of his career into a long pageant of three-score years and ten. Instead, it offers a portrait in time, tracing his appearance through nearly forty years, followed by a portrait in space, offering an idea of what it would have been like to be Mr Pepys' companion about the year 1670.

So we begin with the man himself, and his physical features from the ages of thirty-three to about sixty-seven; and then we return to him as a newly established person of some importance, to see how he had made his way in the world, and what the rich world of Restoration London looked like through his eyes, whether at court, in the theatre or in his own home. The pictures and objects assembled here present all the barriers to understanding that three centuries can throw up. The unconventional form of this catalogue has been devised in order to use as much of Pepys' own descriptions as possible, and thus to diminish the distance between his world and ours.

As so often, our portrait cannot be complete: there are, for example, no more than distant echoes of his work for the Navy. To have shown Pepys' achievements in his professions would have required as much space again. And the reconstruction of his home necessarily includes some pieces later than 1670, though there is almost nothing that does not belong to Pepys' lifetime.

The form of the catalogue precludes detailed notes on each painting giving historical data and critical comment. The list of exhibits and those who have generously lent them will be found at the end, and includes notes as to those paintings which were probably in Pepys' own collection.

RICHARD BARBER

I

A Most Excellent Picture of It

'I do see all the reason to expect a most excellent picture of it,' reflected Samuel Pepys in his diary on March 30, 1666, after he had come home from Mr Hales the painter. He had already sat three times for his portrait [**1, frontispiece**] and was enthusiastic about the result from the very first, but felt that the likeness increased as work progressed. At the outset he had been troubled because 'I sit to have it full of shadows and do almost break my neck looking over my shoulder to make the posture for him to work by', though both the shadows and the pose were in the most fashionable style; then, 'though it will be a very fine picture', he wrote on March 20 that 'I do not fancy that it hath the ayre of my face'. However, all was well, and Pepys paid great attention to the detail, insisting that the music be repainted (a recent X-ray photograph has revealed that the sheet was originally shown falling away at the left) until he was satisfied that it was 'painted true'. He also dissuaded Hales from including a landscape background in the fashionable style, 'though against his perticular mind', because his wife's picture, which had a plain 'sky' or background, seemed more successful. He collected the portrait (and that of his wife, which had been done at the same time [**14**]) on May 23, paid Hales £14 for the picture and 25s for the frame, and hung it up at home 'with great pleasure'.

The earnest, slightly frowning face which Hales elegantly portrayed was that of a man quickly making his way in the world. Son of a tailor of no great wealth, John Pepys of Salisbury Court in Fleet Street, his family had been small farmers in the fens for the past century, rising from monastic

3. Mr Pepys by Greenhill

5. Mr Pepys, c. 1673

servants to masters in a small way of the monasteries' lands during the Reformation. But if John Pepys himself lived in fairly humble circumstances, he had connections in good quarters; and it was to his distant cousin Edward Mountagu that Samuel owed his advancement. Although the family had a largely Puritan tradition, it was the Restoration that made his fortune; as private secretary to Mountagu he was closely involved in the actual return of the King [Part Two, *Great Changes Here*], and obtained office through his master's patronage. At the beginning of 1660, when he started to keep the famous diary, he was living in fairly humble circumstances, having only one servant at the lodgings in Westminster where he and his wife lived. He had married in 1655, perhaps about the time that Mountagu first employed him, Elizabeth St Michel; by any standards it was not a match calculated to further his career, for she was the daughter of the Huguenot Alexander St Michel, a penniless foreigner, and like his daughter, quite impractical. But Elizabeth was precocious and pretty at fifteen and Pepys admitted later 'a strange slavery to beauty, that I value nothing near it' – particularly feminine beauty'. Their married life had not been easy, and they had lived apart for some months, but as Pepys' circumstances became more secure, so his life at home grew easier. Nothing serious was to come between them until later years.

In 1660 they moved from Westminster to Seething Lane, to official lodgings in the Navy Office where Pepys was now Clerk of the Acts. As part of the furnishings of their new apartments, Pepys decided to have their portraits painted, and in November 1661 went to a minor artist, Savill by name, who lived in Cheapside. He was not very happy with the results, and the best praise he could find for the finished work was that it 'do not much displease us', and that 'I did like the picture pretty well'. When he had paid Savill £6 for the two pictures, and 36s for the frames, and hung them up in the dining-room, he thought that 'it comes now to appear very handsome with all our pictures', which confirms the suspicion that this earliest recorded portrait was largely a status symbol. He did like it well enough to sit for 'a picture in little' just after the first was finished.

4. Mr Pepys, c. 1673

6. Mr Pepys by Kneller

The Savill portraits are almost certainly lost, for the two pictures which could be these [4, 5] date from much later. They are not very skilled portraits, and the sitter's age is uncertain. But the details of the larger portrait give a fairly clear indication of the date at which it was painted. Pepys is undoubtedly wearing a periwig, which he first adopted on November 3, 1663; and all the objects surrounding him were bought by him after 1661 – a pair of Joseph Moxon's globes on September 8, 1663, 'for my wife, who hath a mind to understand them' (and another set by the same maker for the office in 1664), 'a pair of tweezers, cost me 14s' (meaning compasses) on June 20, 1662, and a slide-rule on March 25, 1663. As to the guitar, 'methinks it is a bawble', 'so bad an instrument', he says of it in the diary; but he was given an Italian one by the British agent at Leghorn at some time between 1669 and 1671. The instrument here is plainly not the lute which Savill had to paint into the 1661 portrait, but this later gift. The only theory which would dispose of most of these objections is that wig, globe, compasses and rule are all painter's props, designed to express Pepys' new importance as Clerk of the Acts; if so, it is a strangely accurate forecast of the objects which were to become familiar to him, and in any case wigs were scarcely in fashion at all early in 1661.

Pepys was keenly interested in the portrait-painter's art, as both the number of surviving portraits and the diary bear witness. He had watched with interest the progress of Peter Lely, who had come over from Holland shortly after the Restoration: on June 18, 1662, he inspected Lely's studio; Lady Castlemaine's portrait was locked away, so he tipped the artist's servant and said he would come again. When he returned, Lely thought he had come to order a picture and warned him that he was booked up for three weeks, 'which methinks is a rare thing'. He observed the splendid state in which the artist dined, and saw 'the so much by me desired picture of my Lady Castlemayne', of which he bought three engraved copies on December 1, 1666. On another occasion he was critical of Lely's work when drawing the Duchess of York, 'the lines not being in proportion to those of her face', but in general he had a high opinion of his work,

2. *Mr Pepys after Hales*

8. *Mr Pepys after Kneller*

calling his portrait of Lady Carteret 'a very fine picture, but yet not so good as I have seen of his doing'.

It was not to Lely but to his rival Huysmans that he went for a portrait of his wife in 1664; Huysmans was 'said to exceed Lilly', and Pepys found there 'as good pictures, I think, as ever I saw'. But when he went to commission the work on May 31, 1665, he found that the painter was out, and in the end it was John Hales who painted Mrs Pepys as St Catherine a year later [**14**].

He was equally an admirer of Samuel Cooper, the miniaturist. At the height of his career in 1662, Pepys hoped for an introduction to him, but the friends who were to meet him at the coffee-house 'deceived' him; and it was not until March 30, 1668, that Pepys visited him in Henrietta Street. Afterwards, he was moved to declare that 'the painting is so extraordinary, as I do never expect to see the like again'. He had already been persuaded by a friend that he ought to get Cooper to paint his wife's portrait, and he now decided 'that my wife shall be drawn by him when she comes out of the country'. This was duly done in a series of sittings in July 1668; Pepys came to admire Cooper's skill as a linguist and musician, though not entirely happy about the likeness – 'but it is most certainly a most rare piece of work as to the painting'. It cost him £38 3s 4d in all, more than both of Hales' portraits together: but we cannot judge of its relative merits, since both Hales' and Cooper's portraits of Mrs Pepys have disappeared.

Pepys had no other portrait painted before 1670, so the portrait by Hales is our only evidence of what Pepys looked like while he was occupied with his own spiritual self-portrait in the diary, though the copy of it [**3**] may well be that referred to on July 14, 1668: 'This day Bosse finished his copy of my picture, which I confess I do not admire, though my wife prefers him to Browne; nor do I think it like. He do it for W. Hewer, who hath my wife's also, which I like less.' Copies for personal presentation were by no means rare; Pepys sent another to his friend Thomas Hill in Lisbon in 1675, though from which original we cannot tell. Hill's effusive letter of thanks would be more appropriate to a copy of one of the grander, later portraits

7. Mr Pepys by Kneller

9. Mr Pepys by Cavalier

than this more intimate piece: on July 1 Hill wrote: 'The picture is beyond praise; but causes admiration in all that see it. Its posture so stately and magnificent, and it hits so naturally your proportion and the noble air of your face that I remain immovable before it hours together.' This sounds much more like the portrait of about 1670 [3], in which Pepys adopts the same pose as that of his patron the Earl of Sandwich when he was painted by Lely in 1660, for the second time. This is either from Lely's studio or possibly by Lely's imitator J. Greenhill; it shows Pepys as a man of fashion, even though his plumage is, so to speak, borrowed – but he had already hired an Indian gown for the Hales portrait. It is also worth noticing that this almost full-length portrait gives a mere hint of his small stature: he was only a little over five feet tall, and his sensitivity about his appearance may have led to some discreet over-statement on the artist's part.

The pair of small pictures [**4, 5**] are our next evidence of his appearance. Given that our earlier arguments ring true, they can be plausibly attributed to about 1675, as there is some trace of Dutch influence in the large element of still life in the picture. The precision with which the 'tools of his trade' are inserted is probably due to Pepys himself. Pepys had left his old post at the Navy Office, and was now Secretary to the commission which was carrying out the Lord High Admiral's duties. Being a Papist, the Duke of York, later James II (whose trust Pepys had won during the years as Clerk of the Acts), had been forced to retire from the Admiralty in 1673 because of the Test Act, and Pepys organised the department as the new administrative centre for the Navy. The larger portrait, with its air of quiet, unobtrusive efficiency and naval paraphernalia, catches the mood of the period well, if a trifle coarsely compared with the polish of the three-quarter length after Lely [**3**]; the miniature, with its gold anchor frame, seems to be some kind of personal memento, perhaps for his sister Paulina or his brother John, now joint Clerk of the Acts in his place.

Lely's established pre-eminence was challenged in the last years of his life by another Dutchman, Godfrey Kneller,

11. Mr Pepys by Closterman

10. Mr Pepys at the Coronation

who began his career in England about 1675. Soon after Kneller's arrival, Pepys' career suffered a sharp reverse: under suspicion of being involved in a Papist plot, he was sent to the Tower in May 1679 for six weeks, and only cleared of the charges in February 1680: though his accusers had proved false, he remained out of office until 1684. It was probably soon after his restoration to favour that Pepys followed the new fashion in painting, and no less than four versions of this portrait survive. One was presented to the Royal Society to commemorate his Presidency in 1684–1686, though the date of presentation is unknown; one Pepys kept himself, and two copies almost certainly belonged to other members of his family. It seems likely that the version now in the National Maritime Museum [**6**] is the original, painted about 1684–7; the Royal Society version is a copy made very shortly afterwards [**7**], and the versions at Magdalene College, Cambridge, and belonging to Miss T. M. Baumgartner [**8**] are the family copies. Kneller portrays Pepys at the height of his career, recognised not only as a learned virtuoso, but also as a leading administrator, for Pepys was now Secretary to the Admiralty and, in Sir Arthur Bryant's phrase, was proving himself 'the saviour of the navy'. The solemn dignity of the picture is in accord with these great achievements and responsibilities, and the number of copies suggests that it was Pepys' own favourite. Even if it lacks the immediate attraction of the Hales portrait, it is the most rounded of his likenesses. For a truer character, we may turn to the medallion in ivory which Kneller's acquaintance Cavalier carved in 1688 [**9**], which resembles the engraving of him in James II's coronation procession [**10**]. There seems to have been some argument over this, because Kneller had to write to Pepys in January 1690 'upon occasion of some disingenuous dealings of Cavalier the sculptor about his Medall'. Cavalier had apparently asked to do the medallion and was now trying to charge too much and Kneller, in uneasy English, says: 'you will serve him Reight, to pay him 3 Guinis for the wax Cast of from the Equori [i.e. ivory], which he tells me you have, and give him the Equori in telling him you are Contentit wit that aloen.' Pepys evidently decided to keep

12. Mr Pepys by Verrio

the medallion, for it was in the possession of the Pepys Cockerell family until 1931.

There is a sharp contrast between this bold, engaging profile, perhaps the best of all the portraits of Pepys, and the heavy weariness of the Closterman portrait [**11**] painted in the last decade of the century. Much had happened in the interval: with the Glorious Revolution, Pepys had found himself under suspicion of being an active plotter on James's behalf, and had been confined to his house for six days. His connections with James had been too intimate for him to hope to hold office again, though he had hastened to pay his respects to the new ruler, now that his old master had deserted him: Will Hewer wrote to him on December 19, 1688 assuring him of his support and hoping that 'this afternoon or evenings audience will prove to your satisfaction, which I doe heartily wish and pray for, if not, I know you will chearefully acquiesce in what ever circumstance God-Almighty shall think most propper for you, which I hope may prove more to your satisfaction then you can imagine'. All that remained for him, in the words of Sir Anthony Deane (who had found himself in the same situation), was 'the ould soldier's request, a little space between busines and the grave'.

Pepys' retirement was by no means inactive, though his earlier malady of the stone gradually made itself felt again. He had always been an indefatigable collector, and now, with leisure to organise agents abroad, prints and books poured into his library. He corresponded widely, on a vast range of subjects, from second sight to naval antiquities, and amassed materials for a History of the Navy, a project which had grown out of his enquiries into the duties of his office as Clerk of the Acts of which only the 'Memoires relating to the state of the Royal Navy' were published in 1690, though he continued the 'Naval Minutes', his notes on the subject, until 1700. His old association with the Royal Society continued, and its members used to meet informally at 'that Paradise which lookes into the Thames near the Water-gate in York-buildings', as Thomas Gale [**83**] called Pepys' new house. He remained a governor of Christ's Hospital for some years; Verrio's great fresco there,

13. Mr Pepys, possibly a posthumous portrait

14. Mrs Pepys after Hales

painted in 1682–5, includes his portrait (in a scarlet alderman's gown which he had borrowed for the occasion on February 17, 1682, from Sir Thomas Beckford) [12]. But the details of educational administration bored and troubled him, and he gradually gave up his active part there, preferring instead to offer a critique of Dr David Gregory's scheme for a new method of teaching mathematics, into which he wished to see introduced perspective and music, two old interests of his own. It is in this guise, as an enquiring searcher after truth, that the late, even posthumous, portrait perhaps by Thomas Murray rather crudely depicts him [13]; no far cry from the earnest lover of the arts who gazes out at us from Hales' picture of almost fifty years earlier. And, when all is said and done, it is the Hales portrait by which Pepys himself will be best remembered.

The portraits of Mrs Pepys failed to survive the century and a half between her death and the publication of the diary, with one exception, that by John Hales. Either the Savill or the Cooper miniature would have been more interesting, but now one would be only too delighted to find the original of Thomson's engraving [14], which, according to a family legend, was destroyed by a prudish Scottish nurse in the 1830s. It may yet survive, and prove to be a little less bland than the over-polished rendering of the engraver. It is even less vigorous by contrast with the memorial bust from St Olave's Church [15], carved by John Bushnell soon after her death in 1669, possibly from a death mask. Pepys had it placed by the altar, so that it faced across to his habitual seat in the Navy office pew; and it is a remarkably vivid piece of work, as distinctive a bust as the Restoration produced. It tallies with Pepys' portrait of his wife in the diary: gay, pretty, headstrong yet devoted, but not entirely practical, a foil rather than a counterpart to her more down-to-earth husband.

Pepys continued to live at the Navy Office until it was burnt down in 1673; and in that year he was appointed to the Admiralty post, which would have entailed his departure in any case, so that the household in Seething Lane came to an end. His next home for any length of time was that at York House, already referred to, which he shared with his

15. Memorial of Mrs Pepys

16. Mr Hewer

erstwhile clerk, now valued friend, William Hewer **[16]**, from 1679, and he began to spend long periods at Hewer's country house at Clapham after 1701. John Evelyn the diarist visited him there on September 23, and saw 'a very noble and wonderfully well furnished house, especially with all the Indies and Chinese curiosities anywhere to be met with. The offices and gardens are exceedingly well accomodated for pleasure and retirement.' It was Will Hewer who had mediated between Pepys and his wife when Pepys was caught *in flagrante delicto* with her companion, Deb Willet. He had acted for some weeks as Pepys' chaperon, and he must have carried out this mortifying duty with some tact for Pepys to continue to be so friendly with him. He worked with Pepys in naval matters and on the Tangier question, and made a distinguished career for himself; though arrested with Pepys in 1689, he found a new career as Governor of the East India Company. It was he who was Pepys' executor; together with John Jackson **[17]**, second son of Pepys' difficult sister Paulina, he was responsible for the final arrangement of the Pepysian Library now at Magdalene College, Cambridge. Jackson was in a sense Pepys' adopted son, and they seem to have been very close: Pepys sent him on a grand tour in 1699–1700, and his purchases of prints in Italy were exactly what his uncle wished, though his appreciation of music left something to be desired. Pepys himself was still 'liquorish for news', and would have willingly gone with his nephew if his health had allowed it.

Samuel Pepys died on May 26, 1703, after an illness of some months. His old friend Evelyn [**82**] gave him an elegant epitaph in his diary for that day:

'This day died Mr Samuel Pepys, a very worthy, industrious and curious person, none in England exceeding him in the knowledge of the navy, in which he had passed through all the most considerable offices – Clerk of the Acts, and Secretary to the Admiralty – all which he performed with great integrity. When King James II went out of England he laid down his office and would serve no more. But, withdrawing himself from all public affairs, he lived at Clapham with his partner – formerly his clerk – Mr Hewer, in a very noble house and sweet place where he enjoyed the fruit of his labours in great prosperity, and was universally beloved. He was hospitable, generous, learned in many things, skilled in music, a very great cherisher of learned men, of whom he had the conversation.'

17. Mr Jackson

2

Great Changes Here

One of the impulses which in 1660 led Pepys to begin his diary was the sense that dramatic events lay ahead, and a desire to record his own version of them in the secrecy of his shorthand, where, cautious man that he was, he could express his own opinions in safety. The diary opens with a preliminary note, giving the condition of himself and his family, and goes on to describe the state of politics at the time. In a word, the country was unsettled. Since the death of Oliver Cromwell in the autumn of 1658, there had been no clear leader to whom the common people could look; and however much Cromwell's parliaments might debate new forms of government, leadership was what the mass of people demanded, rather than a model republic. Richard Cromwell, the Protector's son, was no politician, and in the words of a contemporary, 'forsook himself', though many were ready to support him. As in the earlier years of the Commonwealth, it was the Army who decided matters. In May 1659, under Major-General John Lambert [**18**], they restored the Rump Parliament, which had been dissolved in 1653; and Richard Cromwell disappeared from the scene. The Rump proved obstinate, and Lambert, who had been frequently mentioned as a possible successor to Oliver, dismissed it again on October 13. For a brief two months it seemed that he might succeed in his ambitions, but his fellow-officers had other ideas. The Rump was restored yet again on December 26; Lambert, now posted in the North, was told to disband his troops. On January 1, the day that Pepys made his first entry, a new figure appeared in the political arena, the commander of the army in Scotland, General Monck [**19**]. The Scottish army was

19. Lord Generall Monck

18. Maj-Gen Lambert

the most disciplined force in the kingdom, and when Monck crossed the border to confront Lambert, it was quickly obvious that he was the new arbiter of England's fortunes. On January 4, there was 'certain news that Lord Lambert his forces were all forsaking him', and on the 5th, as Monck approached, the Rump voted for the election of members to replace those dismissed in 1648 and 1649, and the moderate leaders of those years returned to an active part in politics, the chief among them being General Fairfax [**20**].

Although it was becoming clear that royalist feeling was beginning to sway events, and that a free parliament might well restore the King, Monck had not yet made up his mind to organise elections. Pepys thought him a 'dull, heavy man', and he seems to have been a painstaking and loyal figure rather than a decisive leader in a crisis. All kinds of theories of government were afoot, and the town was alive with rumours and denials of rumours. Pepys himself, on January 9, joined John Harington's republican debating club, but the paper Harington had just published [**21**] was out of tune with the trend of events, and the club broke up on February 21 after some 'exceeding good argument' in the meantime. After this, Pepys remained very cautious about his own position; he records events in the diary, but rarely offers an opinion: of the pamphlets now appearing, such as 'The Loyal Subjects Teares, For the Sufferings and Absence of their Sovereign Charles II' [*22*], he says no more than that they are 'well-writ'. The London mob were less passive: Monck was their St George, the Rump a dragon to be slain. Vicious satires on the Rump were rife, like the ingenious one in the form of a pack of cards [*23*], and when on February 11 Monck ordered the Rump to dissolve by May 6, the Londoners were delighted. That evening, Pepys watched the celebrations [**24**]: 'But the common joy that was everywhere to be seen! The number of bonefires . . . and all along burning and roasting and drinking for rumps – there being rumps tied upon sticks and carried up and down. The butchers at the maypole in the Strand rang a peal with their knifes when they were going to sacrifice their rump . . . indeed, it was past imagination, both the greatness and the suddenness of it.'

20. Sir Thomas Fairfax in council

24. Rump Bonfire

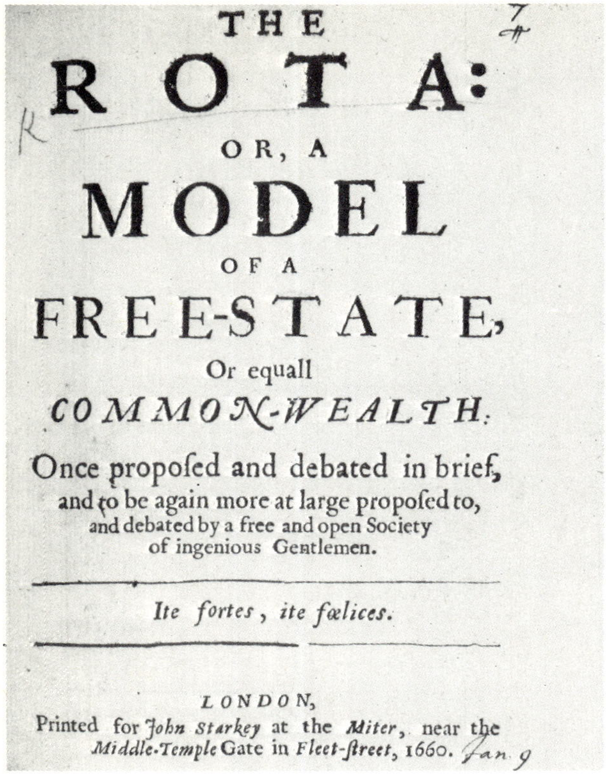
THE
ROTA:
OR, A
MODEL
OF A
FREE-STATE,
Or equall
COMMON-WEALTH:
Once propoſed and debated in brief,
and to be again more at large propoſed to,
and debated by a free and open Society
of ingenious Gentlemen.

Ite fortes, ite fœlices.

LONDON,
Printed for *John Starkey* at the *Miter*, near the
Middle-Temple Gate in *Fleet-ſtreet*, 1660.

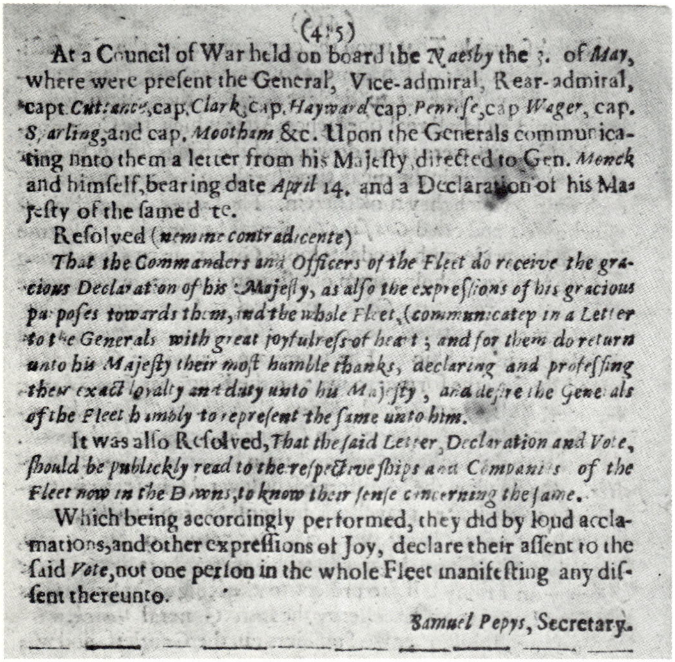
(415)

At a Council of War held on board the *Naesby* the 3. of *May*, where were preſent the General, Vice-admiral, Rear-admiral, capt *Cuttance*, cap. *Clark*, cap. *Hayward* cap. *Penroſe*, cap *Wager*, cap. *Sparling*, and cap. *Mootham* &c. Upon the Generals communicating unto them a letter from his Majeſty, directed to Gen. *Monck* and himſelf, bearing date *April* 14. and a Declaration of his Majeſty of the ſame date.

Reſolved (*nemine contradicente*)

That the Commanders and Officers of the Fleet do receive the gracious Declaration of his Majeſty, as alſo the expreſſions of his gracious purpoſes towards them, and the whole Fleet, (communicated in a Letter to the Generals with great joyfulneſs of heart; and for them do return unto his Majeſty their moſt humble thanks, declaring and profeſſing their exact loyalty and duty unto his Majeſty, and deſire the Generals of the Fleet humbly to repreſent the ſame unto him.

It was alſo Reſolved, *That the ſaid Letter, Declaration and Vote, ſhould be publickly read to the reſpective ſhips and Companies of the Fleet now in the Downs, to know their ſenſe concerning the ſame.*

Which being accordingly performed, they did by loud acclamations, and other expreſſions of Joy, declare their aſſent to the ſaid *Vote*, not one perſon in the whole Fleet manifeſting any diſſent thereunto.

Samuel Pepys, Secretary.

It was Pepys' cousin, Edward Mountagu [25], for whom he acted as agent in London, who finally decided the nature of Pepys' involvement in the political scene. On February 23, Mountagu was chosen a member of the Council of State under Monck, and a week later was named General of the Fleet. Mountagu had held this post from 1656 to 1659, but had compromised himself the previous summer by moving in support of the abortive royalist rising in August. Pepys, although his master's chief source of information on the course of events during his absence from London, seems to have been pursuing his own ends up till now; but this was to change radically when Mountagu appointed him his secretary on March 6.

Although Mountagu's early career had been as one of Cromwell's colonels, and he had served on the Council of State from 1653 onwards, he seems to have been a convinced if necessarily secret royalist by the time he returned to politics, disillusioned by the squabbles of the Commonwealth leaders after the Protector's death. Now that there were 'great hopes of the king's coming again', secrecy was less and less required. Mountagu's exact part in the negotiations was not entirely clear to Pepys, who seemed to be ignorant of his contact (via his eldest son) with the royal court in exile in Holland. These exchanges had been going on since the previous summer, and during April, Pepys, now with the fleet anchored off Deal, noted many comings and goings. On the 21st, he remarked on the presence of various gentlemen, 'formerly great Cavaliers', and a messenger from Mountagu's son with a letter 'with command to deliver it to his own hand. I do believe that he doth carry some close business on for the king.' The Declaration of Breda [*26*], setting out Charles's promises as to the form of government if he returned, and read to Parliament on May 1, was therefore by no means unexpected, though none the less welcome – 'the happiest May-day that hath been many a year to England'. When it was read to the assembled sailors of Mountagu's fleet, the seamen hailed it with delight, though some of the commanders, fearful of losing their places, accepted it reluctantly. As Mountagu's secretary, it was Pepys' signature that appeared at the end of the

21. Mr Harington's Rota

27. Mr Pepys' report

eport in the *Faithfull Post* for May 8 [27]; and part of his etter to an acquaintance was printed in the *Mercurius Publicus* on the same day: 'Then might you see the Fleet in ıer pride, with pendants loose, Guns roaring, Caps flying, ınd loud *Vive le Roy*'s ecchoed from one Ships company to ınother'.

Three days later, the fleet set sail from Dover for Scheveningen Bay [*28*], outside the Hague, where they ınchored during the night of May 13–14 to await the King. Pepys lost little time in disembarking and seeing the sights, hough it was not until May 17 that he actually saw the King himself. Charles II, after long years of uncertain exile, potential embarrassment to any government that sheltered ıim, was now enjoying the first respects to be paid to his ıew status. The quiet domestic life of his penurious days 29] was replaced by triumphant entries, banquets and leputations. From Breda, where he had been since mid-April, the King went via Delft [**30**] to the Hague [**31**] on May 16, where he was feted at a banquet and ball [**32**] on May 20. Bad weather delayed his departure: Pepys had dificulty getting aboard on the evening of the 20th, reporting hat 'This hath not been known, four days together such weather at this time of year, a great while – endeed our leet was thought to be in great danger, but we found all vell.' The Dukes of York and Gloucester were able to come ıboard on the 22nd; the King, having taken leave of the Dutch Estates [*33*], left the Hague [**34**] on the 23rd and mbarked, 'where I in their coming in kissed the Kings, Queen and Princesses hands'. A great concourse of spectators watched the royal departure [**35**], with 'infinite shootoff of the guns, and that in a disorder on purpose, which vas better then if it had been otherwise'.

Pepys found the King that afternoon in a 'very active and tirring' mood, walking up and down the quarter-deck. But t was not unnatural, now that his misfortunes were at an nd, that his mind should run back over the events of the past years. Pepys himself must have been reminded of the lay on which he saw Charles I [**36**] beheaded, contrasting ıis schoolboy enthusiasm for the republican cause then, vith his new-found monarchist views. But the King avoided

25. Mr Edward Mountagu

35. The King departs from Scheveningen

29. The King in exile

30. The King at Delft

31. The Batavian Court

32. The King at The Hague

such painful topics, preferring instead to talk of his escape from Worcester, which Pepys was to record in detail some twenty years later; his shorthand notes taken at the King's dictation in 1680 are one of the main sources for the story [37]. Hearing his account of the refuge in the oak-tree at Boscobel [**38**], and of his escape on horseback as Mrs Lane's servant [**39**] from the King's own lips, Pepys felt 'ready to weep to hear the stories that he told of his difficulties that he had passed through'; not the least of them had been that of crossing the Channel, where the master of the *Surprise* recognised him, and the secret had to be kept from the ship's company. As a memento of that earlier crossing, Charles was to commission a painting of the coal-brig, renamed the *Royal Escape* [**40**].

The voyage was swift, with 'a fresh gale and most happy weather', and the royal flotilla anchored off Dover on the evening of the 24th. The king landed the following morning, and 'the shouting and joy expressed by all is past imagination'; or as Dryden more pompously put it in *Astraea Redux*:

'And now times whiter Series is begun
Which in soft centuries shall smoother run;
Those Clouds that overcast your Morne shall fly
Dispell'd to farthest corners of the sky . . .
O Happy Age! Oh times like those alone
By Fate reserv'd for great *Augustus* Throne!
When the joint growth of Armes and Arts foreshew
The World a Monarch, and that Monarch You.' [*41*]

For Pepys, a humbler homecoming (but no less busy, as the terseness of his diary entries shows) was in store; he remained with the fleet, landing at Deal on June 8, and meeting his wife in London on June 10. It was not long before the rewards for the voyage were distributed: Mountagu had already been made a Knight of the Garter, and Pepys had received £30 out of a bounty of a thousand ducats allocated to his ship. Mountagu, confirmed in his place at court, and about to become Earl of Sandwich was now in a position to offer real rewards to Pepys (who duly had his patron's portrait copied later in the year [**42**]). He

36. The late King at his trial

39. The King as Mrs Lane's servant

promised Pepys the lucrative naval post of Clerk of the Acts. Pepys' friends had already noticed his rise in the world. Pepys notes a letter from Mr Blackburne on March 25, 'who with his own hand superscribes it to *S.P. Esqr.* of which I was not a little proud.' As Pepys dined with a friend on June 25, he might well be 'amuzed [i.e. astonished] at our great changes here'.

Not least of the changes was the reintroduction of royal pageantry; and Pepys, though he found attendance at court 'infinite tedious', was always a lover of spectacle. He watched a damp procession on July 5, when 'the King and Parliament being to be intertained by the City today with great pomp', the rain 'bedaggled many a fine suit of clothes.' (He himself walked up and down Whitehall all morning, afraid to get his new coat wet.) It was ten months before he saw the King again, once more in ceremonial procession; but this time it was for the long-awaited coronation. On the eve of the coronation, April 22, there was a great pageant from the Tower to Whitehall through the triumphal arches erected in the City [44], and despite Pepys' fears, the weather proved fine and he had an excellent view of it all from a house in Cornhill [43]:

'. . . it is impossible to relate the glory of that this day – expressed in the clothes of them that rid – and their horses and horse-cloths. Among others, my Lord Sandwich.

Imbroidery and diamonds were ordinary among them.

The Knights of the Bath was a brave sight of itself. And their Esquires, among which Mr. Armiger was an Esquire to one of the Knights. Remarquable was the two men that represent the two Dukes of Normandy and Aquitane.

The Bishops came next after the Barons, which is the highest place; which makes me think that the next parliament they will be called to the House of Lords. My Lord Monke rode bare after the King, and led in his hand a spare horse, as being Master of the Horse.

The King, in a most rich imbroidered suit and cloak, looked most nobly. Wadlow, the Vintner at the Devil in Fleet-street, did lead a fine company of Souldiers, all young comely men, in white doublets. There followed

40. The Royal Escape

42. My Lord Sandwich

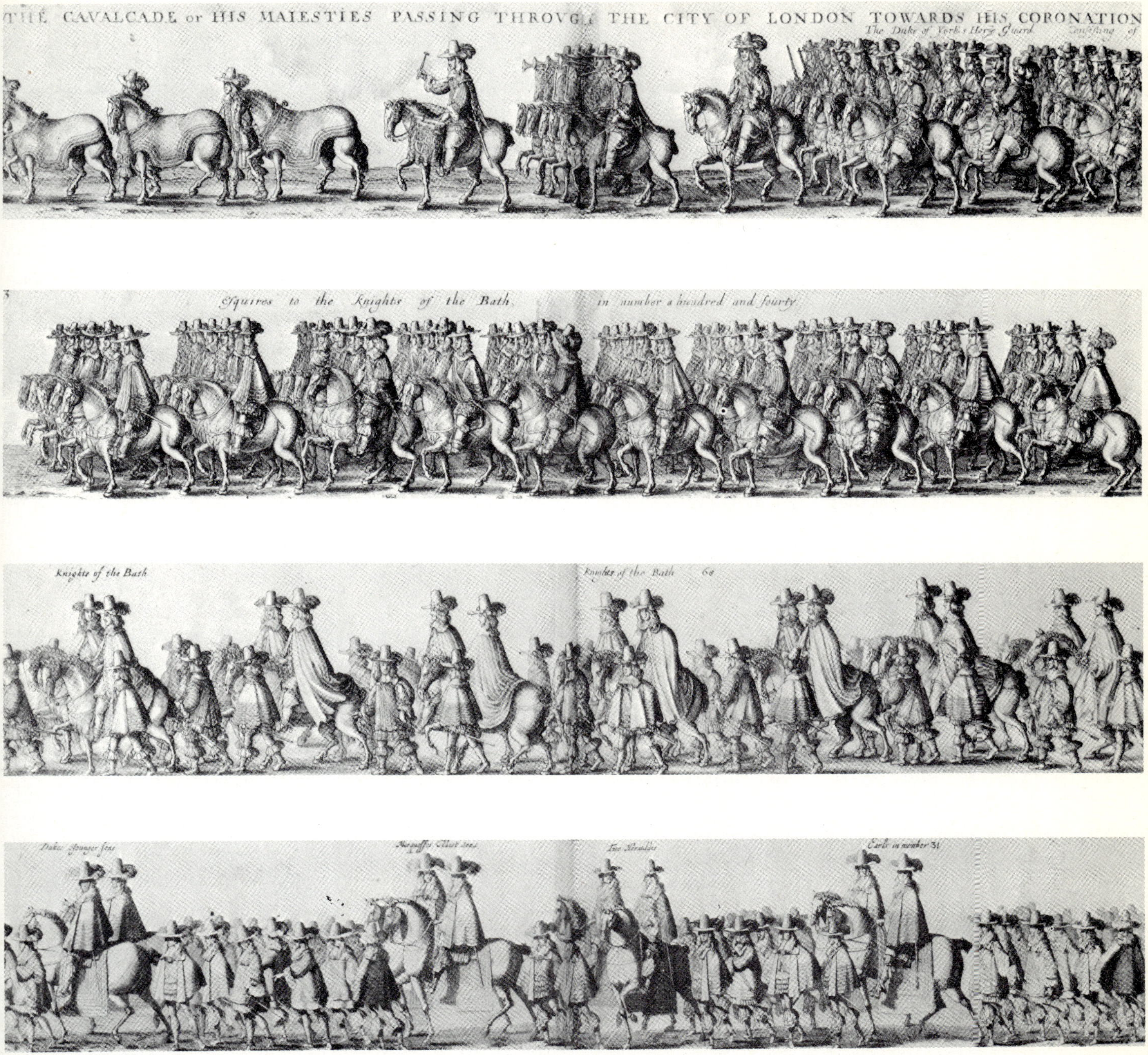

43. Coronacion day

the Vice-Chamberlin, Sir G. Carteret, a company of men all like turkes; but I know not yet what they are for. . . .

So glorious was the show with gold and silver, that we were not able to look at it – our eyes at last being so much overcome with it'.

The following day, Pepys managed to get a perch in a scaffolding in the north end of Westminster Abbey, where he sat from 4 a.m. until nearly midday in order to watch the coronation itself [**45**], or rather, such of the ceremony as he could see: he was also disappointed in the music, which was difficult to hear because of the noise made by the congregation. He contrived to slip out in time to watch the procession to Westminster Hall [*46*], in which the King walked under a canopy held by the Barons of the Cinque Ports, a duty which he was to perform twenty-five years later at James II's coronation [**10**]. He watched with avid interest the ceremonies of food-tasting and of the King's champion's challenge at the banquet that followed, concluding his account of the day: 'Now after all this, I can say that besides the pleasure of the sight of these glorious things, I may now shut my eyes against any other objects, or for the future trouble myself to see things of state and shewe, as being sure never to see the like again in this world.'

44. Triumphal Arch

45. The Coronacion

43. Coronacion day

48. The Queene

The coronation was also the apogee of Charles' popularity. There was a vast gulf between Verrio's 'Sea Triumph of Charles II' [**47**] and his real reputation. Pepys himself had no great respect for him, chiefly because he did not seem to know how to apply himself to the matter in hand. It was not the King's pleasure-seeking in itself that he condemned, but that the King should be dining with Lady Castlemaine and hunting moths while the Dutch were burning his fleet in the Medway, or that he should be seen scrambling over Frances Stuart's garden wall. Pepys, and many others with him, wanted a king they could respect; instead, they found they had a man who disliked ceremonial, allowed his boon companions from his days in exile to take liberties with him, and though naturally intelligent and astute, appeared to care very little for business. In fact, informal meetings and private consultations allowed him much more scope for manœuvre with his ministers, and his financial position at the beginning of the reign was enough to cripple the most able monarch. Nor was he lethargic but took much physical exercise. His wide interests, including science, were renowned, and he took especial note of naval affairs: in both these fields Pepys could admire a fellow-enthusiast, only to find that he was little more than a dilettante. A bare six years after the coronation, Pepys wrote 'How fickle is this man, and how unhappy we [are] like to be!' and the following year he was complaining of the King's 'silly discourse' at the theatre about one of Lord Rochester's amorous exploits.

The Commonwealth had had its moments of glory, and Cromwell had been as great a ruler as any in Europe. The contrast for Pepys was therefore not between a genuine republican leadership and a monarchy, but between two styles of government. Cromwell, though crowned in effigy after his death, had ruled only by virtue of his own talents; and in a sense the same quest for a capable leader had brought about the Restoration. In Charles' early portraits, however formal and however impressive the trappings of state, the artist is looking at the man and not the king. It is only in a later piece by a foreign artist, Verrio, that the full extent of the change is apparent. Charles never won the hoped-for renown which Verrio glorified in 'The Sea Triumph of Charles II', part of the grandiose decorations at Windsor, away from London's republican eyes. The picture underlines all the more forcefully the weakness of Restoration monarchy: appealing to Divine Right, the privileges were accepted, but the responsibilities were neglected.

Charles, though fond of Catherine of Braganza, probably regarded her as one of his responsibilities. She appears chiefly in Pepys' pages either because she was rumoured to be about to produce the heir whom the country so urgently needed, or because her Portuguese entourage and its ways aroused his curiosity. She was brought to England by Lord Sandwich in May 1662, with a large Portuguese retinue, and remained to some extent a foreigner throughout her life, though she learnt to speak 'very pretty English' by January 1664. Although she was by no means the centre of attention at court, she could none the less set a fashion: and Huysmans, the Dutch painter who had recently arrived in England, owed much of his success to her. His portrait of her as St Catherine [**48**] set a fashion copied by many ladies of the court; it was on account of one of these pictures, of Lady Peters, that Mrs Pepys adopted the pose for her portrait by John Hales [**14**], though Pepys had already seen the original, calling it 'most like and most admirable'.

The greatest change of all for Pepys was the arrival of the court itself. Accustomed to the dry arguments of Commonwealth leaders and their entourage, his keen ear for political intelligence now found that scandal was replacing intrigue as the subject for gossip. Who had dined last night with the King? Whose influence was uppermost at court? And, as if this was not enough, there were the wild doings of the courtiers to titillate the ear as well. Pepys was particularly interested by Charles' first favourite, Barbara Villiers, wife of the Earl of Castlemaine and later Duchess of Cleveland. From the day in July 1661 when he 'filled his eyes with her' at the theatre, he always noted her doings, and was loud in praise of her portrait by Lely, which he called 'the so much by me desired picture of my Lady Castlemayne, which is a most blessed picture and that that I must have a copy of'. To which portrait Pepys refers is uncertain, as Lely painted

49. My Lady Castlemaine

47. The Sea Triumph of Charles II

her several times: among the various poses were those as a Madonna with one of her illegitimate children by Charles [**49**], as St Catherine, and as the Repentant Magdalene. Pepys saw this last picture at Hinchingbrooke, Lord Sandwich's home, in July 1664; and as soon as Faithorne engraved the pose as the Magdalene, Pepys bought three copies (December 1, 1666), having tried to get an advance impression the previous week [**81**].

Lady Castlemaine did not go without rivals for long, despite her knowledge of 'all the tricks of Aretin' (the Italian pornographer). Charles was soon in pursuit of the chaste Frances Stuart, later Duchess of Richmond. Despite rumours that she had become the King's mistress in 1663, and the formation of a 'committee . . . for the getting of Mrs Stewart for the King', she remained a 'cunning slut', as Pepys unfairly puts it, and he records in 1667 that she had only once yielded to the King, after her marriage that year, and had at once left the court. She did not find such favour in Pepys' eyes as in the King's, though he admired her picture by Huysmans 'in a buff doublet like a soldier' [**50**] when he visited the painter's studio, as well as John Roettier's medal of her: '. . . the King's new Medall, where little, there is Mrs Steward's face as well done as ever I saw anything in my whole life, I think: and a pretty thing it is, that he should choose her face to represent Britannia by [**51**].' The medal was probably struck at the same time as the full-length pose as Britannia; the latter, first used on a naval medal, became the original for the Britannia which appeared on the copper coinage from 1672 onwards. But he was most taken with her when he glimpsed her at Whitehall in 1664: 'there comes out of the Chayre-roome Mrs. Steward in a most lovely form, with her hair all about her eares, having her picture taking there. There was the King and twenty more I think, standing by all the while, and a lovely creature she in this dress seemed to be.'

Pepys might glimpse Charles and his mistresses at Whitehall or at the theatre, and, in later years, speak with the King on business; but the court itself remained an alien world, the haunt of characters such as 'my Lord Buckingham' [**52**] whose wild doings provided Pepys with some entertaining

51. Mrs Stewart

52. My Lord Buckingham

gossip, though he occasionally professed horror at the court's depravity. Despite his wildness both in morals and politics, Buckingham could charm his way into the King's favour again after lying in the Tower under suspicion of treason. Dryden described him in the satire *Absalom and Achitophel* as Zimri:

'A man so various, that he seem'd to be
Not one, but all Mankinds Epitome.
Stiff in Opinions, always in the wrong;
Was every thing by starts, and nothing long:
But, in the course of one revolving Moon,
Was Chymist, Fidler, States-Man and Buffoon:
Then all for Women, Painting, Rhiming, Drinking;
Besides ten thousand freaks that dy'd in thinking.'

Buckingham was no great friend of Lord Sandwich, Pepys' patron, and on one occasion had threatened to impeach him in the Lords. Pepys was relieved when his political career came to an end after his scandalous seduction of the Countess of Shrewsbury: 'I shall not be much sorry for it, that we may have some sober man come in his room to assist in the Government.'

Henry Bennet, later Earl of Arlington [53], Buckingham's associate in the Cabal of 1667, was a courtier more of Pepys' sober taste: a good patron to his protégés, he once took the trouble to warn Pepys of a plot to deprive him of the Tangier Treasurership, though Pepys dismissed this as mere rumour and did nothing. Setting the two engraved portraits of Arlington and Buckingham side by side, one might (Arlington's scar apart) apply Buckingham's verses on Arlington's portrait equally well to either:

First drawn an arrant Fop, from top to toe,
Whose very Looks at first dash show him so:
Give him a mean proud Gait, a dapper Face,
A pert dull Grin, a black-patch cross his Face,
Two goggle-Eyes, so clear, tho' very dead,
That one may see, thro' them, quite thro' his head . . .'

Arlington and Buckingham, as members of the Cabal, were the sworn enemies of the leading figure of early

50. Mrs Stewart

54. My Lord Clarendon

55. The Duke of York

53. Sir H. Bennet

Restoration politics, Edward Hyde, Earl of Clarendon. The portrait after Hanneman [54] was painted during the royal exile, when he was acting as Charles' secretary, and he reaped due reward on the King's return with an earldom, the post of Lord Chancellor and the unofficial position of chief minister. As such, he at once aroused opposition: Pepys heard as early as July 1661 that he was 'much envyed', and that 'many great men do endeavour to undermine him'. However, 'the King (though he loves him not in the way of a companion, as he doth these young gallants that can answer him in his pleasures) yet cannot be without him for policy and service'. The 'great differences there are at court' continued throughout Clarendon's tenure of power, and he was, according to Sandwich, 'irrecoverably lost' in April 1663. However, the King's support meant that he survived, as great as ever, and when Pepys found himself in Clarendon's disfavour in July 1664, because a Navy Board official had marked trees in Clarendon Park for felling, it was with fear and trepidation that he went to make amends: after dinner on July 14, he 'accosted him, telling him that I was that unhappy Pepys that had fallen into his high displeasure', and arranged to see him that evening. The interview went well, and Clarendon accepted Pepys' excuses. Pepys still had to 'do him service in it', although Clarendon had carefully avoided any specific orders or requests. Glad to escape so lightly, Pepys' official conscience still pricked him: 'Lord, to see how we poor wretches dare not do the King good service for fear of the greatness of these men.' When the Cabal forced Clarendon to flee the country in 1667, Pepys' only comment was that 'he was a man not to be advised, thinking himself too high to be counselled'.

Only two men of standing at court earned Pepys' admiration: Sir William Coventry and James, Duke of York. As Lord High Admiral, James and Pepys had much business to transact; yet Pepys' keen criticism of those he had to work with rarely found fault with him. The respect was mutual: the Duke congratulated Pepys on his good management of the victualling account in 1666, and he came to rely on him for many Navy Office matters. In particular, he supported

Pepys' efforts at Navy reform in 1668. Although James was debarred from office by the Test Act of 1673, and out of touch with naval affairs for a decade, he remembered Pepys when he returned to office in 1684, and made him Secretary to the Admiralty. The two men seem to have been relatively intimate: James gave Pepys several personal presents, including a fine gaming table, and the portrait by Kneller [55]; it is said that he was sitting for this when news of William of Orange's landing reached him. Had James put up any resistance, Pepys might well have been one of his right-hand men, not for political so much as personal reasons.

James' first marriage, to 'Nan' Hyde, daughter of the Earl of Clarendon, was one of the first scandals at court after the Restoration; James' conduct otherwise was discreet compared to his brother's behaviour. Anne Hyde had been a Maid of Honour to his sister, the Princess of Orange, and James had seduced her while the court was in exile in Holland. They were married secretly in November 1659, and it was only when she became pregnant that James avowed the match, in September 1660. Pepys was not well supplied with gossip for once, because on October 10 he was told by Lord Sandwich at dinner that James had stolen the documents from her 'cabinet' and was refusing to marry her, when the public admission had been made a month earlier. Sandwich was speaking French so that the servants should not understand; one suspects that Pepys did not quite catch the story either. The court gradually accepted the match, but the new Duchess was a strong character, and not without enemies: in 1668, she was said to lead the Duke 'by the nose'. Pepys found her proud and extravagant, and, what was perhaps worse, plain; though he admired her portrait by Lely [56]: 'we saw, among other rare thing, the Duchesse of Yorke her whole body, sitting in state in a chair in white Sattin.'

The other courtier who earned Pepys' admiration was Sir William Coventry [57]. Coventry, as secretary to the Duke of York, had not been very much more highly placed than Pepys in 1660, and his career, based on honesty and ability rather than intrigue, was not unlike Pepys' own. As Navy

57. Sir Wm. Coventry

56. The Duchess of York

Commissioner, he was closely associated with Pepys' work, but his reputation was largely made in the Commons, where he was reputed the best speaker in the House. Pepys pays continual tribute to his integrity, and records a conversation with him in October 1662 when Coventry declared that 'he was resolved, whatever it cost him, to make an experiment and see whether it was possible for a man to keep himself up in Court by dealing plainly and walking uprightly without any private game a-playing. In the doing whereof, if his ground doth slip from under him, he will be contented; but he is resolved to try . . .' This directness and honesty led him into conflicts with Lord Sandwich, but he was the kind of man who commanded his opponent's respect, as Clarendon's praise of him bears witness. Coventry's friendship with Pepys was a matter of mutual respect and trust rather than intimacy; in July 1665, just after he had been knighted, Pepys was a little troubled to find that he was 'too great not tó expect to much familiarity with', though no less kind. But in the Restoration court, such a man could not survive long; Charles found him a 'troublesome man', probably because he was too honest to acquiesce in royal mismanagement. His enemies' chance came in 1669, when he challenged Buckingham to a duel over a threatened satire on him in a new play; Charles had him committed to the Tower, and though he was released soon afterwards, he refused to accept any further public office.

Such, then, were some of the leading figures in the new political and social order in which Pepys found himself. There were other, closer associates near to his own social level, particularly at the Navy Office: Sir George Carteret, Sir William Pen and Sir William Batten who figure largely in the pages of the diary; but, they, like Pepys, were the men who had benefited from the 'great changes', rather than part of those changes themselves. It is Pepys' keen interest in the doings of the wider circle of the court, where the change from Commonwealth days was greatest, that we have tried to portray here; and we turn to a field which would scarcely have existed under the Commonwealth: the theatre.

Of the painters whom Pepys admired, he mentions and describes Lely and his work most frequently; but the intimate art of Samuel Cooper [**58**] drew his enthusiastic praise as well. Cooper might have figured more frequently in the diary if a promised introduction to the artist in January 1662 had not failed to materialise. Cooper had been established in London since 1642, but the return of the court brought him a new clientele, and spurred him on to produce his finest work. He was more expensive to commission than Lely: Lely, with a studio and assistants to finish the details, asked only £15 for a bust, while Cooper asked £30. Pepys, even in the prosperous days of 1668, found this dear, and Henry Harris (the actor) had to persuade him before he decided to commission Cooper to paint Mrs Pepys: 'though it cost £30, yet I will have done', he concludes. On the following day, March 30, he went to visit 'the great painter' in his house in Henrietta Street. Here he found much to delight his connoisseur's eye: 'his work . . . is all in little, but so excellent, as though I must confess I do think the colouring of the flesh to be a little forced, yet the painting is so extraordinary, as I do never expect to see the like again. Here I did see Mrs Stewards picture [**60**] as when a young maid, and now again done just before her having the smallpox; and it would make a man weep to see what she was then, and what she is like to be, by people's discourse, now. Here I saw my Lord Generalls picture [*59*], and my Lord Arlington and Ashlys, and several others . . . Being infinitely satisfied with this sight, and resolving that my wife shall be drawn by him when she comes out of the country, I away . . .' Mrs Pepys sat for her portrait early in July; and on close acquaintance Cooper proved to be 'a most admirable workman, and good company'. Pepys admired his 'great skill in music' on his next visit, and declared him roundly to be 'an excellent man'. When, a month later, the work was completed, Pepys cavilled a little at a fancied lack of resemblance and weak handling of the drapes, but decided that it was 'most certainly a most rare piece of work, as to the painting'. Alas, we cannot judge for ourselves, since the miniature does not appear to have survived.

60. Mrs Stewart

58. Samuel Cooper

61. Sir Wm. Davenant

3 The Pleasure of the Play

For Pepys, always eager for novelty, or as he puts it, 'with child to see any strange thing', Restoration London offered many pleasures undreamed of in Commonwealth days. One of the chief of these, for a man who was especially partial to music and beautiful women, was the theatre, where, to the horror of the Puritans, actresses now trod the boards for the first time. The ordinances against public shows had already been breached in Cromwell's time by Sir William Davenant [**61**] and others. Both clandestine performances and public masques had had an eager following throughout the dour rule of religion, and as early as May 1656, Davenant had begun to provide regular performances at Rutland House of 'entertainments' and 'the first English Opera', *The Siege of Rhodes*, was given there in September of that year. Though it lacked the ballets which were a feature of French opera, and differed greatly from Italian stage works in the same genre, Davenant's piece was a great success; and by July 1658 he was able to reopen the theatre which he had used before the Civil War. The turbulent politics of the following year led to a period of closure in March, and Davenant was arrested as a Royalist in July, an episode which stood him in good stead when he rejoined the King in Holland in March 1660. It was not until October of that year that plays resumed in earnest. Davenant had joined forces with Sir Thomas Killigrew [**62**], Charles' Master of the Revels during the exile, and another playwright of experience, to obtain a monopoly of the London theatre, a privilege which they could both claim under earlier royal patents. The two companies which they set up under this arrangement constituted London's only sources of theatrical entertainment for the whole of Charles II's reign, save for occasional incursions by French and Italian players.

Pepy's first visit to this new entertainment was made shortly after the theatres had reopened, on October 11: '. . . in the park we met with Mr Salsbury, who took Mr Creed and me to the Cockpitt to see *The Moore of Venice*, which was well done. Burt acted the Moore; by the same token, a very pretty lady that sot by me cried to see Desdimona smothered.' In the space of the next nine years, he was to see well over a hundred plays; and playgoing became such a passion that he was constrained to make vows against going to the theatre at some time in September 1661; he had been no less than nine times in the previous month, and on September 8 recorded that he was 'troubled in mind to think how much of late I have addicted myself to expense and pleasure'. Yet on the 11th he went to *Twelfth Night* 'against my own mind and resolution', and on the 25th 'much against my nature and will (yet such is the power of the Devil over me I could not refuse it) to the Theatre . . .' His vow was one of moderation rather than total abstinence, and he was generally successful in keeping to his allotted ration, though at Michaelmas 1662 the period of his oath expired, and he was back at the playhouse the next day: likewise at Christmas he was back again as soon as the three months were up. At other times, he kept the letter rather than the spirit of his vow, though he paid his self-imposed penalty of a crown into the church poorbox on several occasions for exceeding his allocation. Having abstained entirely from playgoing between June and December 1663, he relaxed the terms of his oath, and gradually became a regular playgoer again, though he was never so assiduous as he had been in 1661. He was as much concerned with the expense as the loss of time: twelve visits to the theatre, he reckoned, cost about 50s, and on one occasion, when his companion paid for him, he did not hold it to be a breach of his oath. The loss of time could be serious: to secure a seat at a new play, as Pepys found on May 18, 1668, he might have to wait two hours or more. The performance usually began at 3.30 and ended after 6,

63. Major Mohun

so what would today be an evening out was for Pepys an afternoon's business left undone.

The richness of Restoration theatre, with its heritage from Elizabethan and Jacobean playwrights enlarged by the new ideas from the Continent, is too vast a subject to be explored in any detail here. Pepys himself saw a wide range of plays and players; all we can show of the succession of spectacles which he enjoyed are a handful of scene designs and a small number of portraits of stage personalities.

Among the first actors whom Pepys saw was Major Michael Mohun [**63**], who had already acted for Sir William Davenant's company before the Civil War, and had made a great reputation: 'Mr Sheply and I to the new Play-house near Lincolnes Inn fields (which was formerly Gibbon's tennis-court), where the play of *Beggers' bush* was newly begun. And so we went in and saw it. It was well acted (and here I saw the first time one Moone, who is said to be the best actor in the world, lately come over with the King); and endeed it is the finest play-house, I believe, that ever was in England.' The new playhouse was the Theatre Royal, and Mohun, besides being one of its leading actors, had some hand in its management as well. He was an experienced player, having first appeared on the stage about 1624; and he had endured much hardship in the Royalist cause, including thirteen months' imprisonment. A favourite of Charles II, he was called by Rochester the 'great wonder of the *English* stage'; and he seems to have attracted a number of young actors who imitated his style in tragedy, though he himself took tragic and comic leading roles indiscriminately. Pepys did not think so well of him in 1668; he compared his performance as Iago unfavourably with that of Walter Clun, who had met a tragic end four years earlier. The present portrait seems to date from just after his resumption of an acting career; there is a military air about him, though it has been suggested that it portrays him as Cethegus in that favourite heroic drama, Ben Jonson's *Catiline his Conspiracy.*

Pepys' own preference was for Thomas Betterton [**64**], the star of the rival company, Sir William Davenant's players at the Duke's House, also near Lincoln's Inn Fields. He was Mohun's junior by at least twenty-five years, and

62. Sir T. Killigrew

64. Mr Betterton

68. Nell Gwyn

66. Mr Harris

the foremost of the new generation of actors who first appeared after the Restoration. As a manager, Betterton took great interest in the new mechanical techniques of the French theatre, and was responsible for introducing them into Davenant's new building. But it was in his acting that he excelled: Colley Cibber, remembering the latter end of his career (he continued to act until shortly before his death in 1710), said of him: 'I never heard a Line in Tragedy come from *Betterton* wherein my Judgment, my Ear and my Imagination were not satisfy'd'; and of his stage presence he remarks: 'He seemed to seize the Eyes and Ears of the Giddy and Inadvertent'. Pepys admired him in Massinger's *The Bondman* and in *Hamlet* (in which he 'did the Prince's part beyond imagination') in 1661; and he constantly refers to him as the yardstick by which lesser players are to be measured. After the actor's long illness in 1667–8, Pepys was 'glad to see Betterton' again, and praised his Hamlet once more as 'the best part, I believe, that ever man acted'. His sober, low-voiced style was perhaps too restrained for the court, but he was undoubtedly the most popular and consistent tragic actor of the period.

Turning to the comedians, Pepys first records John Lacy [triple portrait, *65*] playing the part of M. Galliard, a dancing master, in May 1662; a curious coincidence, because Lacy had earlier been a professional dancing master. He appears in this part in the centre of the portrait. Lacy, like Mohun, was a shareholder in the Theatre Royal under Killigrew, and adapted French plays for that company. A versatile performer, he ran into serious trouble in 1667 for inserting *ad lib.* comments into his part when acting before the King. The play was Edward Howard's *The Change of Crownes*, and Lacy 'did act the country-gentleman come up to Court, who doth abuse the Court with all the imaginable wit and plainness, about the selling of places, and doing every thing for money. The play took very much.' The next day Pepys learned that the King had forbidden Killigrew's players to act again, being 'so angry at the liberty taken by Lacy's part to abuse him to his face'. Pepys, knowing court life all too well, adds: 'and it was bitter endeed, but very true and witty.' Lacy himself was imprisoned, but five days ater 'by great intercession, released from his durance under he groom porter, where he stood committed by his Majesty's order for having on his own head added several ndiscreet expressions in the part he acted in a late play'. The other costumes in which he is shown in the triple portrait are probably Sawney the Scot in his own adaptation of *The Taming of the Shrew* (Sawney being Petruchio) and Scruple, the canting nonconformist minister in John Wilson's *The Cheats.* But the part in which Pepys most admired him was that of Teague in Sir Robert Howard's *The Committee.* He found Lacy 'beyond imagination' in this farcical part as an Irish footman in June 1663; four years ater, 'Lacy's part is so well performed that it would set off anything'.

Among Pepys' acquaintances was Henry Harris, of the Duke's Playhouse, who had started as a scene-painter, but soon turned to acting instead. He first appeared with Davenant in November 1660, and Pepys admired his performance in Lord Orrery's *Henry V*, a part in which he was ater to have him painted by John Hales. This picture is lost, but Greenhill's fine drawing of him as Cardinal Wolsey in *Henry the Eighth* survives [**66**]. The costume, despite Davenant's particular care for detail in this production, is a mixture of Roman Catholic and Protestant styles, but none he less striking enough. Pepys came to know Harris well n later years; on January 24,1667, he dined with Pepys, at what proved to be an evening 'of the merriest enjoyments I must look for in this world'. He had had a brief *tête-à-tête* with Harris in his closet; 'and I find him a very curious and understanding person in all, pictures and other things,—and a man of fine conversation'. The two soon became good friends, and Pepys' admiration grew with each meeting: 'I was mightily pleased with his company', he declared on another occasion after dining with him. He did, however, have reservations about finding himself with Harris in theatrical company, which included some of the court rakes as very rogues as any in the town': 'But Lord! what loose cursed company was this that I was in tonight; though full of wit and worth a man's being in for once, to know the nature of it and their manner of talk, and lives.'

67. Mr Cartwright

Pepys was always quick to notice a good actor who wa not so well known as stars like Harris, or to remark on speech well delivered. Though he was not impressed b William Cartwright [67] when he saw him as Falstaff i 1660 soon after he had joined Killigrew's company, h noted his good performance of the speech 'What i Honour?' in the same part seven years later. Cartwright who had turned bookseller during the Commonwealth had acted before the Civil War, and with Lacy and Mohu was one of the few links with the Jacobean theatre. Thi handful of players had worked both with the 'boys' and th 'women'; for the greatest single change that the interva brought about was the arrival of actresses to grace th boards (and scandalise the Puritans). This was probably a innovation of Sir Thomas Killigrew's, in December 1660 when Margaret Hughes played Desdemona, and thoug 'boys' such as Edward Kynaston took women's parts for little longer, the feminine triumph was soon complete.'

Pepys viewed these novel and flamboyant creatures wit mixed feelings. He found them most attractive – too attrac tive, indeed – but could not quite repress a more sever judgement on their morals. Going up into the dressin rooms on October 5, 1667. to see his friend Mrs Knipp he met Nell Gwyn 'dressing herself, and was all unready and is very pretty, prettier than I thought' – perhaps not little like the portrait here [68]. 'But Lord, to see how the were both painted would make a man mad – and did mak me loathe them – and what base company of men come among them, and how lewdly they talk.' He first mention 'pretty witty Nell' when he finds her sitting next to him i the theatre in 1665, not many months after she had starte to act, but he had watched her on the stage the previou August in *Flora's Vagaries*, when she gave a 'most ingenuou performance of the young jade Flora'. He followed he fortunes with interest, and was sorry to learn in 1667 tha Lord Buckhurst had lured her away from the stage t become his mistress: 'Poor girl! I pity her; but more th loss of her at the King's House.' Many of his anecdotes c her are rightly famous, such as the episode when 'Nelly an Beck Marshall, falling out the other day, the latter called th

69. Miss Davis

72. Jacob Hall

73. The Great Fire

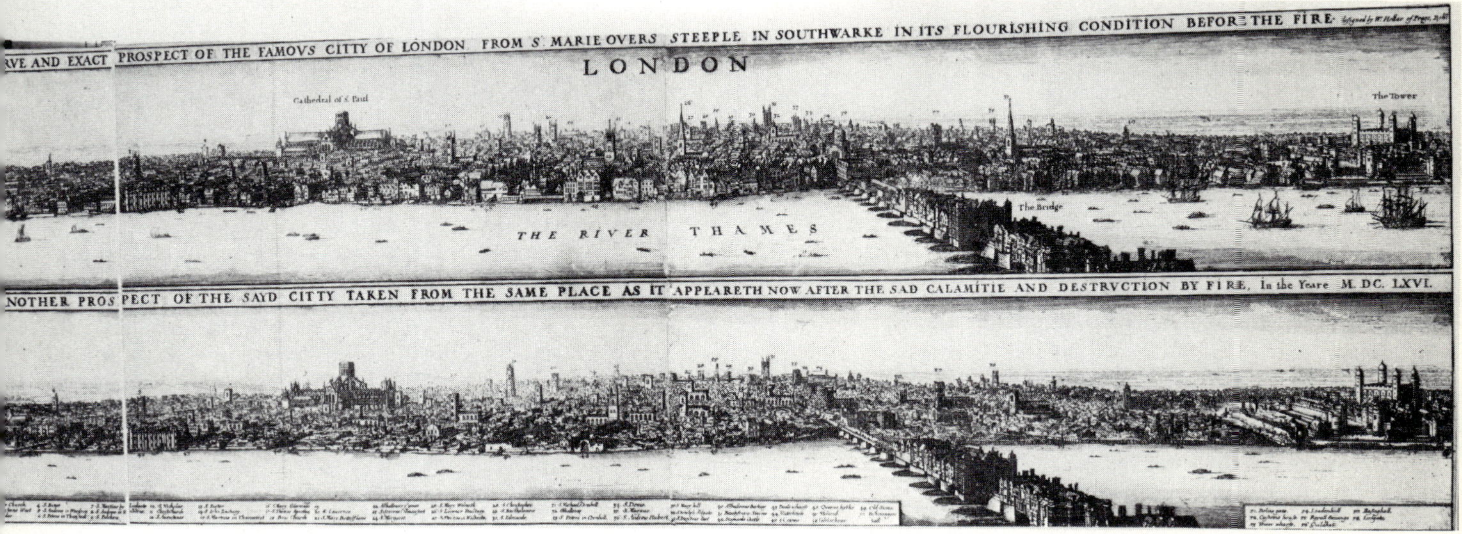

other my Lord Buckhurst's whore. Nell answered that, "I was but one man's whore, though I was brought up in a bawdy-house to fill strong waters to the guest; and you are a whore to three or four, though a Presbyter's praying daughter!" – which was very pretty.' He admired her, rightly, as a comic actress, but, like Nell herself, knew her lack of talent in tragedy. Even her dancing, despite Buckingham's declaration that he

'dreads the strut and mien
Of new-prais'd poets, having often seen
Some of his fellows, who have writ before,
When Nell has danc'd her jig, steal to the door,
Hear the pit clap, and with conceit of that
Swell, and believe themselves the Lord knows what',

Pepys recognised as being less accomplished than that of her rival Moll Davis of the Duke's Playhouse. Indeed, it was more for her own sake than as an actress that Pepys remarked on her, whether 'standing at her lodgings door in Drury-lane in her smock sleeves and bodice, looking upon one', or in a theatre box, 'a bold merry slut, who lay laughing there upon people'.

Pepys' admiration for Moll Davis [69] was in a different vein: himself an accomplished musician, he appreciated her fine singing, and her dancing was one of the great attractions of Davenant's company. Flecknoe, in his poem to her 'on her Excellent dancing', called her:

'Dear Mis: delight of all the nobler sort;
Pride of the Stage and darling of the Court,
Who wou'd not think to see thee dance so light,
Thou wert all air? or else all soul and spirit?'

Her most famous part was in Davenant's *The Rivals*, which according to John Downes had 'a very Fine Interlude in it, of Vocal and Instrumental Musick, mixt with very Diverting Dances', evidently designed as a vehicle for her. Her part as '*Celia*, a sheperdess being Mad for Love' included the song 'My Lodging it is on the Cold Ground': 'She perform'd that so charmingly, that not long after, it Rais'd her from her Bed on the Cold Ground to a Bed Royal.' Pepys notes the King's habit of taking actresses as his mistresses and comments sadly: 'very mean, methinks, in a prince and I am sorry for it – and can hope for no good to the state from having a prince so devoted to his pleasure.'

Such were a few of the stars of the Restoration theatre whom Pepys admired; what would one not give for a portrait of Pepys' personal favourite, Mrs Knipp? Equally there is little to show what a Restoration performance looked like. The designs for Lord Orrery's *Mustapha* [70] by John Webb (a pupil of Inigo Jones) are in the earlie[r] tradition of Jacobean masques, but were a novelty in the theatre proper. As Flecknoe says, 'they were but plain and simple, with no other Scenes, nor Decorations of the Stage but onely old Tapestry, and the Stage strew'd with Rushe[s] (with their Habits accordingly) whereas ours now for cos[t] and ornament are arriv'd at the heighth of Magnificence'. The production of *Mustapha* was particularly elaborate and so costly that it had to serve for several other plays, as note[s] in the prompter's copies show. In particular, the Queen of Hungary's chamber [top right] served for Lord Orrery's *Guzman* in 1669.

For an idea of a performance in progress, we must turn to the engravings in Elkanah Settle's *The Empress of Morocc[o]* (1673), showing the interior of the newly built Dorse[t] Garden Theatre, designed by Sir Christopher Wren [71]. In the opening scene, the music room in the 'heaven' to either side of the royal arms and the beams for suspending chandeliers to light the stage can be clearly seen (the latte[r] are immediately below the top of the proscenium arch). The dramatic torture scene in Act V underlines the appetit[e] of Restoration audiences for realistic spectacle, howeve[r] gruesome.

The theatre alone did not satisfy Pepys' observant and enquiring nature. He was always ready to go and watch an interesting sight, whether it were a gambling den or a side show at a fair, such as the famous rope-dancer Jacob Hal[l] [72], whom he watched at Bartholomew Fair in Augus[t] 1668: 'a thing worth seeing and mightily followed'. A month later, he saw the performance again at Southwar[k] Fair: 'And thence to Jacob Hall's dancing on the ropes

70. Designs for Mustapha, *1666*

Act Five, Finale: Here the Scene Opens and Crimalhaz appears cast down on the Gaunches being hung on a Wall set with spikes of Iron.

where I saw such action as I never saw before, and mightily worth seeing. And here took acquaintance with a fellow that carried me to a tavern, whither come the music of this booth, and by and by Jacob Hall himself, with whom I had a mind to speak to hear whether he had ever any mischief by falls in his time; he told me, "Yes, many; but never to the breaking of a limb." He seems a mighty strong man.'

It was an event in real life, however, that called forth all Pepys' powers of description and provided the pages of his diary with more drama and spectacle than any theatre. His account of the Great Fire of 1666, though written later in the year from loose notes, has a vividness which Evelyn's more ponderous and reflective style lacks. Pepys conveys the urgency and bustle of the crisis, and by sketching individual scenes, brings home the size of the disaster. He was one of the first to bring the news to Whitehall once the seriousness of the fire was realised: 'and there up to the King's closet in the chapel, where people came about me, and I did give them an account dismayed them all; and word was carried in to the King. So I was called for, and did tell the King and Duke of Yorke what I saw, and that unless his Majesty did command houses to be pulled down nothing could stop the fire. They seemed much troubled, and the King commanded me to go to my Lord Mayor from him, and command him to spare no houses, but to pull down before the fire every way.' But action was not so

71. The Empress of Morocco

Act One, Scene One: A Dungeon

Act Two, Scene One: The Prospect of a large River with a glorious Fleet of Ships

Act Two, Scene Two: A Moorish Dance is presented by Moors in several Habits, who bring in an artificial Palm-tree

Act Four, Scene Two: A Hell, in which Pluto, Proserpine and other Women spirits appeared seated, attended by Furies

W. Doll

easily organised: 'At last met my Lord Mayor in Canning Streete, like a man spent, with a handkercher about his neck. To the King's message he cried, like a fainting woman, "Lord, what can I do? I am spent. People will not obey me. I have been pulling down houses. But the fire overtakes us faster than we can do it.".' This was at about eleven on Sunday morning, September 2; the fire had only destroyed a small and densely packed area on the riverside, but the fierce easterly wind began to fan it out in a wider and wider arc. Despite the efforts of the King himself on the following day, it continued to spread north and west; and by nine o'clock on Tuesday evening, St Paul's was surrounded. Shortly afterwards, the huge decaying church was ablaze, and it is this, the most dramatic moment of the fire, that the three pictures record. The large panel [73], which is the finest surviving view of the Great Fire, is probably based on a sketch made at the time from a boat near Tower Wharf. From left to right, the buildings are: Old London Bridge (Nonesuch House and Chapel House and other buildings on it), St Dunstan-in-the-West and St Bride's, All Hallows the Great and then Old St Paul's. Between the Cathedral and the Tower are St Magnus Martyr, St Lawrence Pountney spire, St Mary-le-Bow and St Dunstan-in-the-East, the last on fire. This painting and one of the small panels [*75*] show Old St Paul's still unharmed, a dark silhouette in the ring of fire, while a variation [*76*] shows the burning of St Paul's in progress.

Pepys was more concerned with the slow progress of the fire against the wind towards his home in the Navy Office. His solution, thought out on the afternoon of September 4, 'sitting melancholy with Sir W. Penn in our garden, and thinking of the certain burning of this office', was to send for workmen from Woolwich and Deptford. But a letter to Sir William Coventry produced no reply, and the fire reached the bottom of his lane the next morning, though some efforts had been made the night before: 'Now begins the practice of blowing up of houses in Tower-street, those next the Tower, which at first did frighten people more then anything; but it stopped the fire where it was done . . .' At the approach of the fire Pepys 'took my gold (which was about £2,350), W. Hewer and Jane, down by Poundy' boat to Woolwich. But Lord, what a sad sight it was b moonlight to see the whole City almost on fire – that yo might see it plain at Woolwich, as if you were by it.' He di not hope to find his home intact on his return: 'my con fidence of finding our office on fire was such, that I durst no ask anybody how it was with us, till I came and saw it no burned'. Sir William Penn had organised the workmen a Pepys had suggested, and had blown up houses to goo effect. All that remained was to beat out isolated fires roun the edge of the devastated City, and to survey the desolatio depicted in Hollar's engraving [77]: 'the saddest sight c desolation that ever I saw'. But Pepys' own home and good were safe, the sum of his losses in these dramatic days bein about '£20 cost one way or others, besides about £2 charge in removing my goods'. With most of one of th world's great cities in smoking ruins, he had indeed escape lightly.

4

And So Home

'he household and its contents which Pepys laboured so ıard to save from the Great Fire are mirrored in minute letail in the pages of the diary. Pepys regarded the furnishıng of his household as an excellent investment, and was ontinually at work improving, altering and adding to his ›ossessions. He did not own the house he lived in: soon ıfter he started the diary, in July 1660, he moved into the ›fficial lodgings in the Navy Office to which his new posiion as Clerk of the Acts entitled him. The Navy Office, in ›eething Lane near the Tower of London, was housed in ıalf of a great house which had belonged to Sir Francis Valsingham. How large it was we cannot tell, for it only ›scaped the Great Fire to be burned down early in 1673; he only surviving engravings of the Navy Office depict ›ir Christopher Wren's subsequent rebuilding of it. There vere forty-eight hearths in it, according to the tax return or 1666, but it housed half a dozen officers and provided heir business quarters as well. From the references in the liary, Pepys' part seems to have been a two-storey building, vith a cellar, and three or four rooms on each floor. In the ourse of his improvements, Pepys added a storey to the ıouse in collaboration with his neighbour (in the summer of 662), put a new staircase in the parlour, and enlarged the ıall. It is difficult to discover exactly how many rooms there vere, as Pepys is apt to call the same room by different ıames as he pleases. The ground floor probably consisted ›f the hall, dining-room, parlour and kitchen; above that, here were perhaps his study and his wife's closet; on the ıext floor, their bedroom and a dressing room, and the naids' quarters in the attics.

80. Page from Pepys' print collection

79. Oak bookcase, contemporary with and identical to Pepys' own

The interiors of the rooms were basically Jacobean, the building itself being Tudor. The walls, probably wainscoted in oak, were decorated by Pepys with a variety of hangings, the most striking being tapestries and gilded leather. The latter he put in the dining-room in October 1660; it may have been embossed in the Dutch fashion, and, with green serge curtains, he pronounced it 'very fine'. In 1669, he altered the decoration by getting Danckerts, the landscape painter, to do views of Greenwich and Hampton Court. It was only in 1668 that he could afford tapestries, ordering the 'second suit of Apostles' for £83, to hang in the best chamber, with one or two pieces to spare for elsewhere, rather than the 'best suit' costing £80 for three pieces only. Other rooms were hung with chintz (in his wife's study), counterfeit damask and 'red hangings' (in a bedroom); only the closet proved difficult, Pepys fearing that the purple he had chosen would be 'too sad for that melancholy room' – it evidently had little outside light – but he solved the problem by covering the wall over the chimney with mirrors, in imitation of Philip Howard's room in Whitehall Palace.

Pepys' old lodgings in Axe Yard had been relatively small, so he had to buy a good deal of furniture. His first major purchase was a dining-table to seat ten people, which cost him 50s in January 1663; entertaining played a very large part in Pepys' life, and he was now able to do so in style. In April of that year he entertained seven friends to his great annual feast to celebrate his successful operation for the removal of kidney stones in 1658, and recorded that they were 'very merry before, at, and after dinner, and the more for that my dinner was great and most neatly dressed by our own only mayde. We had a Fricasse of rabbets and chicken – a leg of mutton boiled – three carps in a dish – a great dish of a side of lamb – a dish roasted pigeons – a dish of four lobsters – three tarts – a Lampry pie, a most rare pie – a dish of anchoves – good wine of several sorts; and all things mighty noble and to my great content.' Three years later he bought a set of three chairs and a couch for the substantial sum of £40; these were for his parlour, to which his guests would repair after dinner. Other improvements to

78. Mr Pepys' Library at Buckingham Street

82. Mr Evelyn

this room in later years included a new chimney-piece made for him by Simpson the joiner, and the set of tapestries already mentioned.

The room to which he paid special attention was his closet or study. Its lack of light was made worse by the accumulation of books and papers, which even Pepys' methodical nature could not keep from confusion as he worked. The chaos eventually drove Pepys to a drastic solution. Books were usually kept in coffers rather than on shelves, though some large libraries used what were known as 'presses'. Pepys, as an avid collector, had far more books than were to be found in an ordinary household, and therefore copied the libraries' usage. On July 23, 1666, 'comes Simpson the Joyner; and he and I with great pains contriving presses to put my books up in: they now growing numerous, and lying one upon another on my chairs, I lose the use to avoid the trouble of removing them, when I would open a book'. The presses or bookcases so contrived are now to be seen in the Pepysian Library at Magdalene College, Cambridge: as Pepys' library grew, so he added to them, until there were a set of twelve. Two or three – the diary entries are not clear – were made in 1666; each contains about 250 books. The next evidence of the growth of his library is a drawing of c. 1690, which shows his library at 14 Buckingham Street with seven presses [**78**]; and a further five were added by 1705, when John Jackson, as his executor, finally arranged the books and reduced the number to exactly 3,000. The press here [**79**] is almost identical to No. 12 in the Magdalene College set: although the main features of the set are the same, the carpenters who made the later additions introduced slight variations. For example, the shelves in the early cases are adjustable, indicating that Pepys had not yet decided to arrange his library by the height of the books. The system of shelves sliding in grooves cut in the uprights may have been the result of his and Simpson's 'contriving'; but when he had decided on his method of arrangement, there was no further need for adjustment, and the later cases have fixed shelves. Two other curious features are the unusually long front bolt on the top door, devised so that Pepys, a short man, could reach it easily. He still needed the steps shown in the drawing [**78a**, left], to reach the top shelves; and the bottom shelf, containing the folio volumes, was given doors which slid up instead of swinging outwards, perhaps because there was less danger of falling over them in a small room. Quite apart from being the earliest English examples that survive of a bookcase as a separate piece of furniture, Pepys' presses are remarkable witnesses to his ingenuity, attention to detail and insistence on neatness.

Besides his books, his library also contained a large collection of prints mounted in huge volumes and captioned in a neat hand by a secretary [**80**]. A few choice prints and maps were hung on the walls together with oil paintings. He was particularly attached to the print of Lady Castlemaine by Faithorne after Lely (see p. 23) [**81**] which he had varnished and 'the frame done like gold'. Other decorations included 'maps and pictures and draughts': in later life he commissioned two portraits, of his friends John Evelyn the diarist [**82**] and Dr Thomas Gale, Dean of York [**83**], for his library. Pepys met Evelyn (whose epitaph on him has already been quoted, p. 11 above) when the latter was appointed commissioner for the care of sick seamen in September 1665; but Pepys had already walked in Evelyn's garden at Sayes Court in the previous May. They quickly became good friends, both having the same enquiring turn of mind, and were both members of the Royal Society. Evelyn was a little stiffer and more pompous than Pepys, who says that he 'must be allowed a little for a little conceitedness', but bears eloquent witness to his versatility and polish. Dr Gale was another friend from this learned circle; though he and Pepys were both Fellows of the Society, Pepys does not give a pen-portrait of him in the diary. But a warm correspondence in later years bears witness to their friendship, a friendship based on a common love of learning. It was appropriate that his portrait should hang in Pepys' library, and that it should be one of the first of the new genre of 'library-portrait' which became popular in the eighteenth century.

Of the many books mentioned by Pepys in the diary, or associated with him, a handful stand out as being of par-

83. Dr Gale

81. Faithorne's print of Lady Castlemaine after Lely

ticular interest. First and foremost is Lord Bacon's *Faber Fortunae* [*84*] which he read and re-read several times. This essay on ambition and self-help appealed particularly to Pepys; he mentions it seven times between May 1661 and October 1666, the last occasion being when he gave it to his younger brother as an exercise in Latin translation. Perhaps as he grew more successful, this guide to ambition ceased to have the same interest. His later purchases of books tended to be grander than this little volume, and he was particularly interested in illustrated books, such as John Ogilby's description and engravings of Charles II's coronation [**44**] which 'fell to my lot at his lottery' when Ogilby went bankrupt and disposed of his stock. Even so, the coronation book and an Aesop cost him £4 'besides the binding'. Thomas Sprat's *History of the Royal Society* had several interesting features for him: not only was Pepys a member, but the title-page was from a drawing by John Evelyn showing Lord Brouncker, then President [*85*], and an old associate of Pepys' at the Navy Office (though Pepys could never make up his mind about him and called him at different times 'a rotten-hearted, false man as any I know' and 'the best man of them all' at the office). When Pepys in turn became President in 1684–6, he was to put his imprimatur in this capacity on a much more famous book: Sir Isaac Newton's *Principia Mathematica* [*86*]. However, when he himself came to write his *Memoires relating to the State of the Navy* [**87**], political considerations made him leave his name off the title-page, though the text makes it clear enough that he was the author.

Pepys' taste in paintings other than portraits is not so well recorded. He mentions the purchase of a Dutch snow landscape for 40s, but unfortunately leaves the painter's name blank. He certainly bought Danckert's work, as we have seen, and admired Verelst's flower paintings: 'a Dutchman, newly come over, one Everelst, who took us to his lodging close by, and did show us a little flower-pott of his doing, the finest thing that ever I think I saw in my life – the drops of Dew hanging on the leaves, so as I was forced again and again to put my finger to it, to feel whether my eyes were deceived or no. He doth ask £70 for it; I had the vanity to bid him £20 – but a better picture I never saw in my whole life; and it is worth going twenty miles to see.' Pepys returned the next day to repeat his offer, but Verelst would not come down below £50. Realism, even if it was *trompe l'oeil* realism, delighted Pepys: he waxed lyrical over his friend Mr Povey's pictures: 'But above all things, I do the most admire his piece of perspective especially, he opening me the closet door, and there I saw that there is nothing but only a plain picture hung upon the wall.' A year later he was still intrigued by these paintings, 'being strange things to think how they do delude one's eye, that methinks it would make a man doubtful of swearing that ever he saw anything'. The perspectives he describes are probably those by Hoogstraten at Dyrham Park [**88**]. Another artist who must have aroused Pepys' interest in later years was Willem van de Velde; although he never mentions him by name, a small painting by him of 'a Dutch galleott and other vessels in a strong breeze' was sold by his descendants in 1848, and Pepys may have owned a picture similar to the fine example of his work shown here [**89**]. The *Cleveland* yacht was a successor to the *Bezan* and other yachts which Pepys frequently used on his journeys up and down the river.

Another aspect of Pepys' wide interests is more difficult to illustrate: his curiosity about new developments in mathematics, a subject which he held in high esteem. He introduced it into the curriculum of Christ's Hospital, and tried to improve the standard of it in the Navy, with a view to avoiding the disastrous errors in navigation which were all too frequent. Pepys bought a variety of instruments for his own use: compasses, brass square, slide-rule, 'double-horizontal dial' (possibly an astrolabe) and a parallelogram. He was also an amateur of optical experiments: his other acquisitions included a microscope, a scotoscope (somewhat like a camera obscura) and Wren's 'instrument for perspective'. He also experimented with a telescope: 'we endeavoured to see the moon, and Saturne and Jupiter; but the heaven proved cloudy, and we lost our labour, having taken pains to get things together, in order to the managing of our long glass'. Perhaps the best image of Pepys as an enthusiast for such things is the small portrait of him in his study [**4**].

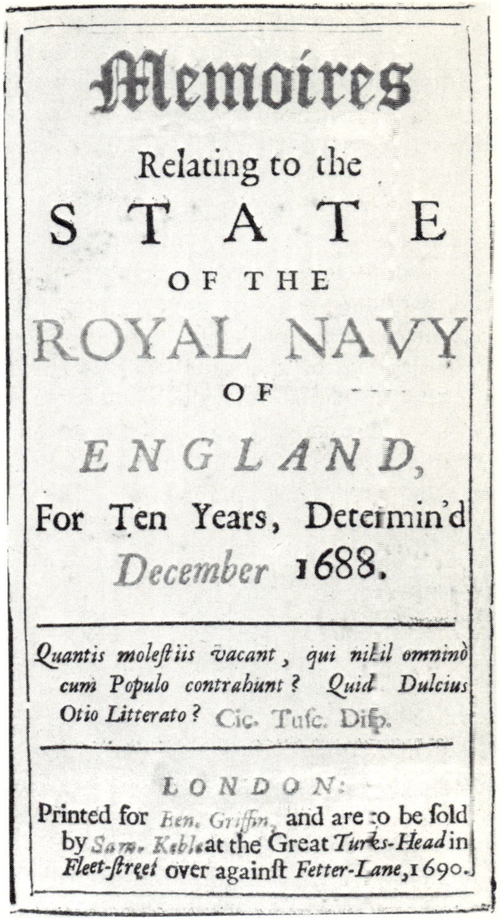

Memoires
Relating to the
STATE
OF THE
ROYAL NAVY
OF
ENGLAND,
For Ten Years, Determin'd
December 1688.

Quantis moleſtiis vacant, qui nihil omnino cum Populo contrahunt? Quid Dulcius Otio Litterato? Cic. Tuſc. Diſp.

LONDON:
Printed for *Ben. Griffin*, and are to be ſold by *Sam. Keble* at the Great *Turks-Head* in *Fleet-ſtreet* over againſt *Fetter-Lane*, 1690.

87. Title page of Pepys' only published work

Before we leave the scene of his private labours and turn to more frivolous matters, the diary itself deserves our attention [*90*]. This little set of six calf-bound volumes of various sizes contains over one and a quarter million words, all written in a neat seventeenth-century shorthand not unlike modern systems, though considerably slower to use. Pepys' original interest in shorthand probably dated from his Cambridge days, when there was some vogue for it; but he seems to have adopted it as much as a means of concealing his intimate thoughts as for his own convenience. All the volumes he used were probably notebooks sold by a stationer, the blocking on the spine being added afterwards as the volumes were filled; the blocking on the front and back dates from the end of Pepys' life when all his plain books were so treated. The manuscript itself is almost always neat and methodical, as he wrote it up from rough notes; though the symbols grew larger as his eyesight began to fail. A long entry could take as much as an hour to write, and many of the hours he spent in his study must have been taken up with this labour of love.

Pepys' enthusiasm was not always directed to such serious ends: we have seen how the theatre could distract him from business, and his love of fine clothes and good food were equally strong. Indeed, the diary presents a magnificent chronicle of his rise in fashion as he rises in the world, from his 'suit with great skirts' which is the first object he mentions, to the gold lace sleeves which aroused such comment in May 1669 that he resolved 'never to appear in court with them, but presently to have them taken off as it is fit I should'. As a tailor's son, and with a younger brother who was a tailor as well, Pepys was a good judge of fine clothes. Indeed, some of his wardrobe was made for him by his brother, such as the jackanapes coat he bought in July 1660. This was presumably for going about his naval business, as it was a grander version of a sailor's close-fitting short jacket. But for all his interest in making a brave show, Pepys never seems to have owned more than half a dozen suits at a time before 1670. Pieces of old suits or other material were frequently used again: in February 1664 he gave his brother-in-law 'a close-bodied light-coloured cloth coat, with a gold edging in each seam, that was the lace of my wife's best pettycoat that she had when I married her'. Two years later, he improvised his court mourning out of 'a new black cloth suit to an old coat', and in June 1667 he turned 'my old silk suit and cloak into a suit and vest'.

The Restoration had brought in its wake all the splendour and extravagance of Continental fashion in the place of the sober suitings of the Commonwealth. At court, the fops vied in spendthrift splendour, and the King himself decreed a new fashion in 1666, though this was to be the fashion to end all fashions: on October 8, Pepys notes that 'the King hath yesterday in Council declared his resolution of setting a fashion for clothes, which he will never alter. It will be a vest [i.e. a long jacket without lapels], I know not well how; but it is to teach the nobility thrift, and will do good.' Alas, it proved a pious hope; Evelyn recorded sceptically ten days later that 'divers courtiers and gentlemen gave his Majesty gold by way of wager that he would not persist in this resolution'; but the unexpected *coup de grâce* was the news in November that Louis XIV 'hath, in defiance to the King of England, caused all his footmen to be put into vests, and that the noblemen of France will do the like; which, if true, is the greatest indignity ever done by one prince to another . . .' Pepys' indignation was perhaps all the greater because he himself had adopted the new style a fortnight before, and had thought well of it – 'I like myself mightily in it, and so doth my wife' – and he feared that his expense had been in vain.

For clothes were elaborate and expensive; a camelot cloak and a velvet coat cost £6 and £8 respectively (when his salary was £350 a year). Pepys might well lament a fortnight later that he 'got a little rent in my new fine camlett cloak with the latch of Sir G. Carteret's door; but it is darned up at my tailor's, that it will be no great blemish to it; but it troubled me'. Pepys had only two workday suits early in 1666, as his remark on January 15 shows: 'Busy all morning in my chamber in my old cloth suit, while my usuall one is to my tailor's to mend, which I had at noon again.' This was probably the 'new fine coloured cloth suit, my cloake lined with plush, as good a suit as ever I wore in my life', made in October 1664. His other suits were too grand for everyday wear, one being black silk and goat's hair costing £34, the other being ferrandin, or coloured silk and wool. These were for Sundays and holidays, though he had a little trouble over the latter on one Sunday: 'Up, and expected long a new suit; but, coming not, dressed myself in my late new black silke camelott suit; and, when fully ready, comes my new one of coloured ferrandin, which my wife puts me out of love with, which vexes me, but I think it is only my not being used to wear colours which makes it look a little unusual upon me.'

Mrs Pepys was just as fond as her husband of dressing stylishly, though Pepys generally spent more money on his own clothes than on hers. Pepys might allow her her 'new fashion pettycoates of sarcenet (fine silk) with a black broad lace printed round the bottom and before', and her 'green petticoat of flowered satin, with fine white and black gimp lace of her own putting on', but if she became too fashionable he grew jealous and suspicious. In 1665 he objected to her 'light-coloured locks, quite white almost, which, though it makes her look very pretty, yet not being natural, vexes me, that I will not have her wear them', and a year later was still not sure that he approved of her 'with a new fair pair of locks, which vex me, though like a fool I helped her the other night to buy them'.

Eventually, in May 1667, she was forced to promise 'to wear no more white locks while I lived'. On the other hand, he found her 'very pretty' in black patches, and bought her a vizard, or mask, both equally artificial fashions. He was also prepared to buy jewellery for her, regarding this as a good investment: in 1666, he spent £80 'upon a necklace with three rows, which is a very good one'.

Mrs Pepys was evidently expected to make some of her own clothes, and did not always succeed too well: Pepys had occasion to find fault with her in May 1667 for appearing in a black moiré waistcoat and short petticoat 'laced with silver lace so basely that I could not endure to see it'. However, on the famous occasion when Pepys wore his gold-laced suit, he found his wife 'extraordinary fine, with

88. Trompe l'oeil interior

her flowered tabby [watered silk] gown that she made two years ago, now laced exceeding pretty; and indeed was fine all over'. Lace, usually of gold or silver, was one of the most expensive trimmings: in December 1668, Pepys spent '£3 or £4 in lace, for her and me'. In earlier years he had had to take old metal lace to the silversmith in order to exchange it for new, and even ordinary lace was very expensive: he records with pride the day in June 1665 when he put on his first 'laced-band, all lace' (a lace cravat).

Indeed, the trimmings were almost as important as the clothes themselves. The most important change in fashion was the adoption of periwigs for general use, which only elderly men had worn under the Commonwealth. The Duke of York took to one in February 1664, and the King followed suit in April. Pepys had experimented with them the previous May: 'After dinner went out to my brother's, and thence to Westminster, where at Mr Jervas's, my old barber, I did try two or three borders and perriwiggs, meaning to wear one; and yet I had no stomach [for it], but that the pains of keeping my hair clean is so great.' He was still without 'great desire or resolution yet to wear one' in August, but finally capitulated on November 3: 'By and by comes Chapman, the periwigg-maker, and upon my liking it, without more ado I went up, and there he cut off my haire, which went a little to my heart at present to part with it but it being over, and my periwig on, I paid him £3 for it; and away went he with my own hair to make up another of, and I by and by, after I had caused all my maids to look upon it and they conclude it do become me, though Jane was mightily troubled for my parting of my own haire and so was Besse. . . . but it is over, and so I perceive, after a day or two, it will be no great matter.' However, the Duke of York commented a week later 'that Mr Pepys was so altered with his new periwigg that he did not know him'. It was not entirely a solution to the problem of cleanliness as Pepys had hoped; in March 1667 he was having trouble with the wig-maker, whose products were 'full of nits, so I was troubled to see it (it being his old fault)'. And there were other unexpected dangers: 'Here I also, standing by a candle that was brought for sealing of a letter, do set my periwigg a-fire, which made such an odd noise, nobody could tell what it was till they saw the flame, my back being to the candle.'

There were unexpected associations, too: going home with his wife on May 12, 1667, 'in our way bethought ourself of going alone, she and I, to a French house to dinner, and so enquired out Monsieur Robins, my perriwig-maker, who keeps an ordinary, and in an ugly street in Covent-garden, did find him at the door, and so we in; and in a moment almost have the table covered and clean glasses, and all in the French manner, and a mess of potage first, and then a couple of pigeons a l'esteuvé, and then a piece of bœuf-a-la-mode, all exceeding well seasoned, and to our great liking.' Next to his appearance, Pepys cared almost as much for his food. On days when little happened, he records what he had had to eat, and the diary gives us a fascinating picture of a Londoner's diet in the seventeenth century. The basic meats were much what one would expect, beef, mutton, and to a lesser extent pork and poultry. Game was common: there was the occasional pheasant, while rabbits, hares and venison abounded, though on at least one occasion Pepys found the venison to be 'palpable beef', to his disgust. Meat was generally roasted, and then served as a hash or as a pie: and the 'umbles' and other parts were all used, such dishes as calf's head, ox's cheek and brawn being frequent. Other items are less familiar: roast swan and hog's harslet appear, as do some unusual fish: lampreys, sturgeon, eels, tench and even a sturgeon and lamprey pie. Lobsters and oysters were two of Pepys' particular favourites, and friends often sent him a barrel of the latter. But not all meals were as interesting as this: staying in a Cambridgeshire inn in September 1663 all he could get was a dish of cold cream for supper and breakfast, and a Lenten dinner might be no more than 'sugar-sops' and fish. Winter food would still be largely salted and preserved, and there was no question of out-of-season delicacies: Pepys usually notes his first plate of oysters of the year, the end of August usually being the beginning of the season, and he also remarks on the first mackerel (April 30) and peas (May 22) of the year in 1664. In hot weather, food was difficult to keep, and on several occasions Pepys abandoned his meal in disgust, despite the sauces and pickles used to counteract this. Sauces were a frequent means of disguising food that was not quite right, and the Duke of York had his own special recipe, 'which he did then eat with every thing, and said it was the best universal sauce in the world, it being taught him by the Spanish Embassador; made of some parsley and a dry toast, beat in a mortar, together with vinegar, salt, and a little pepper; he eats it with flesh, or fowl, or fish'. There were foreign delicacies of other kinds to be tried, such as melons and a Spanish *olio* stew, as well as homely dishes which are now almost forgotten, samphire, mulberries, nettle-porridge and 'poor-jack' or dried salt fish. Tansy (egg-pudding flavoured with tansy) and syllabub were typical sweets, though fruit was more usual.

Other drinks familiar to use were novelties for Pepys. Tea had first appeared from Holland just before the Restoration, and Pepys first drank it in September 1660: 'And afterward did send for a Cupp of Tee (a China drink) of which I never drunk before.' He later found it good for colds, but it remained a rarity, costing about £2 per lb. Chocolate, introduced in 1652, was better known, and Pepys was given a quantity of it by an unknown well-wisher early in 1660. This, too, he regarded as medicinal: after a heavy evening's drinking to celebrate the coronation, he was given chocolate by Mr Creed 'to settle my stomach', his head being 'in a sad taking through the last night's drink'.

Pepys' usual drinking habits were moderate: ale was his everyday drink, usually at midday, though some ale was better than other brews, and he particularly commended those he liked. Brewing was on a small scale, and might often be done by the innkeeper. Wine, on the other hand, was rarely distinguished by its origin; Pepys mentions Château Haut-Brion as being especially good, but he may well have been following the established fashion, which had led to an extraordinary demand for this wine in England. Of fortified wines, he drank sack or sweet sherry, and he also mentions tent (Spanish red wine from Malaga).

Pepys was a man of habit, and his day followed a fairly regular pattern. He would rise just after dawn, and after doing anything necessary at home, or even playing his lute for a while, would spend the morning at the office. Breakfast consisted of a morning draught at about eleven, usually ale, but on other occasions chocolate or a pint of orange juice. Dinner followed at any time between one and five, depending on the time of year; it was the main meal of the day, and guests were frequently invited. The afternoon was less often devoted to work, unless the office was particularly busy: he might go to a play, walk in Hyde Park or go down to Whitehall. In summer another hour or two in the office rounded off the day's business, and he would return home for supper while it was still light. With the three rooms in front of us, we can perhaps imagine him as having had supper and written up his day's entry in the journal. He is out walking on the flat roof behind his house with his wife, singing to his lute in the twilight. In a minute or two, he will come in, go to his dressing room, 'and so to bed'.

89. The Cleveland Yacht

List of Exhibits and Lenders

1. SAMUEL PEPYS

   John Hales, 1666
   Oils on canvas, $29\frac{3}{4}'' \times 24\frac{3}{4}''$
   National Portrait Gallery
   Pepys Cockerell sale, 1848, lot 118, 'Portrait'; put up as 'Portrait of a Musician'

2. SAMUEL PEPYS

   After John Hales, ?1668 or 1675
   Oils on canvas, $29'' \times 24''$
   The Worshipful Company of Clothworkers

3. SAMUEL PEPYS

   After Sir Peter Lely, but possibly by J. Greenhill, c. 1670
   Oils on canvas, $50'' \times 41''$
   The Master and Fellows of Magdalene College, Cambridge

4. SAMUEL PEPYS

   Unknown artist, ? c. 1673
   Oils on canvas, $11\frac{5}{8}'' \times 9\frac{3}{4}''$
   Mrs Ronald Crichton
   Pepys Cockerell sale, 1848, lot 97, 'K. de Moor, *Mr Pepys seated in his Study*'

5. SAMUEL PEPYS

   Unknown artist, ? c. 1673; derived from 4, above
   Oils on copper, $3'' \times 2\frac{1}{4}''$
   Mr R. H. Muir

6. SAMUEL PEPYS

Sir Godfrey Kneller, c. 1682–6; probably the original portrait

Oils on canvas, 29¼″×24¼″

National Maritime Museum

Pepys Cockerell sale, 1931, lot 5. There is a close copy at Magdalene College, Cambridge, and a free version at Yale University Art Gallery

7. SAMUEL PEPYS

After Sir Godfrey Kneller; presentation copy, c. 1686

Oils on canvas, 29″×24″

The Royal Society

8. SAMUEL PEPYS

After Sir Godfrey Kneller, before 1700

Oils on canvas, 24″×29½″

Miss Tryce M. Baumgartner

9. SAMUEL PEPYS

J. Cavalier, 1688

Ivory, 3″ diameter

The Worshipful Company of Clothworkers

Pepys Cockerell sale, 1931, lot 1

10. SAMUEL PEPYS

From *The History of the Coronation of James II*, by Francis Sandford, 1687

Enlargement of detail from engraving

National Portrait Gallery

11. SAMUEL PEPYS

Attributed to John Closterman, c. 1695

Oils on canvas, 28″×22″

National Portrait Gallery

There was a copy of this portrait in the possession of Sir Lionel Cust, 1903; and a copy in poor condition is in the National Portrait Gallery, (2092). This may be 'Mr Pepys's Head by Riley' which is in a MS. list of the Pepys Cockerell pictures, 1824

12. SAMUEL PEPYS

Antonio Verrio, 1682

Fresco (photographic detail)

The Governors of Christ's Hospital

13. SAMUEL PEPYS

Unknown artist, early eighteenth century; possibly posthumous

Oils on canvas, 42″×34″

The Master and Fellows of Magdalene College, Cambridge

14. ELIZABETH PEPYS

I. Thomson, after J. Hales, 1828

Engraving, 5″×3¾″

National Portrait Gallery

Original reputedly destroyed, but possibly Pepys Cockerell sale, 1848, lot 110, as 'Rembrandt School: Portrait of a Lady' (bought in)

15. ELIZABETH PEPYS

Attributed to John Bushnell, 1672

Memorial bust (cast), from St Olave's, Hart Street

National Portrait Gallery

16. WILLIAM HEWER

Sir Godfrey Kneller, c. 1685

Oils on canvas, 29¼″×24¼″

National Maritime Museum

Pepys Cockerell sale, 1931, lot 6

17. JOHN JACKSON

R. Cooper, after Sir Godfrey Kneller, 1828

Engraving, 5¼″×3⅞″

National Portrait Gallery

18. MAJOR GENERAL JOHN LAMBERT

T. Houbraken, after R. Walker, 1739
Engraving, $14\frac{1}{2}'' \times 9''$
National Portrait Gallery

19. GENERAL GEORGE MONCK, DUKE OF ALBEMARLE

Samuel Cooper, c. 1670
Vellum, $4\frac{3}{4}'' \times 3\frac{3}{4}''$
Her Majesty the Queen

20. The manner of His Excellency Sir Thomas Fairfax and the officers of his Armie sitting in council

Unknown engraver, c. 1648
Engraving (photographic enlargement)
The Ashmolean Museum, Oxford

21. 'The Rota; or a model of a free state'

James Harington, 1660
Facsimile of title-page
British Museum

22. 'The Loyal Subjects Teares . . .'

Anonymous pamphlet, 1660
Facsimile
British Museum

23. Satire on the Rump Parliament in the form of playing cards

c. 1659–60
Facsimile
British Museum

24. 'The Rump Bonfire,' February 11, 1660

(A) Anonymous engraving from Samuel Butler, *Hudibras* (1710) (facing p. 146)
(B) Engraving by William Hogarth from *Hudibras* (1726) (facing p. 364)
Photographic enlargements
British Museum

25. EDWARD MONTAGU, later Lord Sandwich

Sir Peter Lely, c. 1659; certainly before June 27, 1660
Oils on canvas, $29\frac{3}{4}'' \times 24\frac{1}{2}''$
Lady Fox

26. The Declaration of Breda

Printed pamphlet, May 1660
Facsimile
British Museum

27. Report of council, of war signed by Pepys

Faithful Post 53, pp. 414–15, May 8, 1660
Facsimile
The Bodleian Library

28. Map of Edward Mountagu's voyage to meet King Charles II, March 27 to May 25, 1660

Based on Chart 3 from G. Collins' *Great Britain's Coasting Pilot* (1696, reissued 1753)
(Chart 5 was dedicated to Pepys)

29. Charles II and the Duke of Gloucester in exile

S. à Bolswert after Gilles Hendricx
Engraving, $13\frac{1}{2}'' \times 17\frac{1}{2}''$
National Portrait Gallery

30–34 Plates from Sir William Lower: A Relation of the voiage and Residence which Charles the II hath made in Holland, 1660

30. The Deputies of the Estates of Holland compliment the King at Delft (May 25)

31. The Batavian Court (i.e. The Hague)

32. The Great Feast the Estates of Holland made to the King and to the Royal Family (May 30)

33. His Majesty taking his leave in the Assembly of the Estates General (June 1)

34. His Majesties Departure from the Hage to his Fleet before Scheveling.

Engravings by T. Philippe after Vrouwliet and Matham
Facsimiles
London Library

35. THE DEPARTURE OF CHARLES II FROM SCHEVENINGEN

Attributed to Johannes Lingelbach, 1660
Oils on canvas, $36\frac{1}{2}'' \times 57''$
Her Majesty the Queen

36. CHARLES I AT HIS TRIAL

Edward Bower, 1649
Oils on canvas, $53'' \times 40\frac{3}{4}''$
Sir John Carew Pole, Bt

37. Pepys' shorthand notes of Charles II's escape, first page

1680
Facsimile
The Master and Fellows of Magdalene College, Cambridge

38. K. Charles II and Coll. Carless, advising under the royal oak

Anonymous, c. 1670
Engraving, $8\frac{1}{2}'' \times 5''$
National Portrait Gallery

39. Charles II and Mrs Lane

M. Vandergucht, after P. La Vergue
Engraving, $10\frac{1}{2}'' \times 6\frac{1}{2}''$
National Portrait Gallery

40. THE ROYAL ESCAPE

Willem van de Velde, c. 1675
Oils on canvas, $25'' \times 30''$
Her Majesty the Queen

38. K. Charles II and Coll. Carles.

41. 'A Proclamation . . . for proclaiming of His Majesty King . . .'

Broadsheet, May 8, 1660
Facsimile
British Museum

42. EDWARD MOUNTAGU, K.G., EARL OF SANDWICH

Emmanuel de Critz, after Sir Peter Lely, 1660
Oils on canvas, 30″ × 24″
Hon. Robin Neville
Pepys Cockerell sale, 1848, lot 24

43. Relation of his Majesty's entertainment passing through London to his coronation, by John Ogilby

Engraved by Wenceslaus Hollar, 1662
A, B, C, D, E: Procession from the Tower to Whitehall (14″ × 18″ each)

44. Relation of his Majesty's entertainment passing through London to his coronation, by John Ogilby

Engraved by Wenceslaus Hollar, 1662
A, B, C: Triumphal Arches in the City ($10\frac{1}{2}$″ × 15″, 10″ × 18″, 11″ × 17″)

45. Relation of his Majesty's entertainment passing through London to his coronation, by John Ogilby

Engraved by Wenceslaus Hollar, 1662
Coronation of Charles II (15″ × 18″)

46. Relation of his Majesty's entertainment passing through London to his coronation, by John Ogilby

Engraved by Wenceslaus Hollar, 1662
Procession from Westminster Abbey to Westminster Hall (15″ × 18″)
National Portrait Gallery

47. THE SEA TRIUMPH OF CHARLES II

Antonio Verrio, 1674
Oils on canvas, $87\frac{1}{2}$″ × $90\frac{1}{4}$″
Her Majesty the Queen

48. CATHERINE OF BRAGANZA AS ST CATHERINE

Jacob Huysmans, 1664
Oils on canvas, $71\frac{1}{4}$″ × $41\frac{1}{4}$″
Her Majesty the Queen

49. BARBARA VILLIERS, COUNTESS OF CASTLEMAINE, AS THE MADONNA

After Sir Peter Lely, c. 1665
Oils on canvas, 69″ × 45″
National Portrait Gallery

50. FRANCES STUART, DUCHESS OF RICHMOND

Jacob Huysmans, 1664
Oils on canvas, $50\frac{1}{4}$″ × 41″
Her Majesty the Queen

51. FRANCES STUART, DUCHESS OF RICHMOND

(A) John Roettier, 1667. Silver medal, $2\frac{3}{4}$″ diameter
(B) After Roettier, 1672. Halfpenny; as Britannia

52. GEORGE VILLIERS, SECOND DUKE OF BUCKINGHAM

Anonymous, after Lely
Engraving, $9\frac{1}{4}$″ × $6\frac{3}{4}$″
National Portrait Gallery

53. HENRY BENNET, EARL OF ARLINGTON

Anonymous, after Lely
Engraving, $9\frac{1}{4}$″ × $6\frac{3}{4}$″
National Portrait Gallery

54. EDWARD HYDE, EARL OF CLARENDON

After Adriaen Hanneman, c. 1648–55
Oils on canvas, 35½″28½″
National Portrait Gallery

55. JAMES II

Sir Godfrey Kneller, 1688
Oils on canvas, 49″ × 42½″
Mrs Claire Pennyman Worsley
Pepys Cockerell sale, 1931, lot 8

56. ANNE HYDE, DUCHESS OF YORK

Sir Peter Lely, 1662
Oils on canvas, 70½″ × 55½″
Scottish National Portrait Gallery

57. SIR WILLIAM COVENTRY

John Riley, c. 1670
Oils on canvas, 59″ × 50″ overall
The Marquess of Bath

58. SAMUEL COOPER

Copy after self portrait
Wash on paper, 6⅛″ × 4⅝″
National Portrait Gallery

59. GENERAL GEORGE MONCK, DUKE OF ALBEMARLE

Samuel Cooper
Oils on paper, 2½″ × 3¼″
The Duke of Buccleuch and Queensberry, K.T., G.C.V.O.

60. FRANCES STUART, DUCHESS OF RICHMOND

Samuel Cooper, c. 1670
Vellum, 4¾″ × 3¾″
Her Majesty the Queen

34. His Majesties Departure from the Hage

61. SIR WILLIAM DAVENANT

William Faithorne, after John Greenhill, 1673
Engraving, 5″ × 4½″
National Portrait Gallery

62. SIR THOMAS KILLIGREW

William Sheppard, 1650
Oils on canvas, 41¼″ × 32½″
National Portrait Gallery

63. MICHAEL MOHUN

British School, c. 1660
Oils on canvas, 29½″ × 25″
Lord Sackville

64. THOMAS BETTERTON

Studio of Sir Godfrey Kneller, c. 1690–1700
Oils on canvas, 30 × 25½″
National Portrait Gallery

65. JOHN LACY in three of his roles

After J. M. Wright, c. 1668
Photographic enlargement of detail
Her Majesty the Queen

66. HENRY HARRIS as Cardinal Wolsey

John Greenhill c. 1664
15½″ × 12¾″
The President and Fellows of Magdalen College, Oxford

67. WILLIAM CARTWRIGHT

John Greenhill, c. 1680
Oils on canvas, 40½″ × 33½″
The Governors of the Dulwich College Picture Gallery

68. NELL GWYNN

Simon Verelst (?), c. 1670
Oils on canvas, 37″ × 29½″
Arnold Wiggins Esq.

69. MARY DAVIS

After Sir Peter Lely, c. 1665–70
Oils on canvas, 49½″ × 40″
National Portrait Gallery

70. Designs for Lord Orrery's *Mustapha*, 1666

John Webb, 1666
Photographic enlargements
The Trustees of the Chatsworth Settlement

71. Engravings from *The Empress of Morocco* by Elkanah Settle

T. Dolle, 1673
Photographic enlargements
British Museum

72. JACOB HALL the rope dancer

British School, c. 1650 (?)
Oils on canvas, 29″ × 24½″
F. T. Dent Esq.
Similar to an engraving of 1792; the identification is traditional, and the combs have not been explained

73. The Fire of London: September 3, 1666, evening

Dutch School, c. 1667–70
Oils on panel, 36″ × 61″
The Trustee of the London Museum
Willem van de Velde has been suggested as the artist

74. Map showing progress of the Fire of London

Based on 'An Exact Surveigh of the streets Contained within the Ruins of the City of London'
Engraved by John Leake, 1669

75. The Fire of London: September 3, 1666, evening

T. Wyck, c. 1667–70
Oils on canvas, 24½″ × 36″
The Duke of Beaufort, K.G.

76. The Fire of London: September 3, 1666, evening
T. Wyck, c. 1667–70
Oils on canvas, $26\frac{1}{2}'' \times 44\frac{3}{4}''$
Mr and Mrs Oliver Millar

77. Parallel views of London before and after the fire
W. Hollar, 1675
Engraving, $23'' \times 17\frac{1}{2}''$
British Museum

78. Drawings of Pepys' library at Buckingham Street
Unknown artist, c. 1690–1700
Photographic facsimile
The Master and Fellows of Magdalene College, Cambridge

79. Oak bookcase
After original by Simpson, last quarter of seventeenth century
Ronald A. Lee Esq.

80. Pages from Pepys' print book
c. 1690
Photographic facsimile
The Master and Fellows of Magdalene College, Cambridge

81. Lady Castlemaine
W. Faithorne, after Sir P. Lely, 1666
Photographic facsimile
The British Museum

82. John Evelyn
Sir G. Kneller, 1684
Oils on canvas, $31'' \times 26\frac{1}{2}''$
Trustees of the Will of the late J. H. C. Evelyn

24 (B). Hogarth's version of the Rump Bonfire

83. Dr Thomas Gale

Sir G. Kneller, c. 1685
Oils on canvas, 29″ × 24″
City Art Gallery, York

84. *Faber Fortunae,* in *Sermones Fideles* by Francis Bacon

Amsterdam 1662
The British Museum

85. *History of the Royal Society* by Thomas Sprat

London, 1667
The British Museum

86. *Principia Mathematica* by Sir Isaac Newton

London, 1686
The British Museum

87. *Memoires relating to the state of the Navy* by Samuel Pepys

London, 1690
The British Museum

88. Interior in *trompe l'œil* perspective

S. Hoogstraten, c. 1660
Oils on canvas
The National Trust (Dyrham Park)

89. *The Cleveland Yacht*

Willem van de Velde the Younger, 1673
Oils on canvas, $11\frac{1}{2}'' \times 19\frac{3}{4}''$
M. S. Robinson Esq.

90. Facsimile of manuscript of the diary of Samuel Pepys

G. Bell & Sons